THE
DEBONAIRE
DISCIPLE

by

DANA PROM SMITH

FORTRESS PRESS   Philadelphia

Library of Congress Catalog Card Number 73–79326
ISBN 0–8006–1036–9

3794C73   Printed in U.S.A.   1–1036

To Marie

"Full of grace and truth"

TABLE OF CONTENTS

PREFACE

A person writes, preaches, and teaches originally out of his own need, else there isn't much point to it. These forms of advocacy stem from a person's attempt to grapple with problems bothering him. A sermon is the minister working through some problem of the faith, and the distinction between a good sermon and a mediocre one is whether he's working through it for the first time or not. A bad sermon is one in which he isn't working through anything in particular.

The problem with which I have been wrestling is the awareness that the traditional forms of piety, or the style of life befitting a believer, are dead. I became dimly aware of this as an adolescent. I was a believer in Jesus Christ but often felt out of place with fellow believers. For a long time I vacillated between feeling guilty and defiant about it. It wasn't until I was in the ministry for some years that I began to get the problem into focus.

Gradually I began mentally to gather bits and pieces of the problem. One of the first was due to a series of lectures by Roland Tapp at Ghost Ranch in which he pointed out that the French translate the word for "meek" in the Beatitudes as "debonaire." That rolled around in my mind and sermons for several years. Then I read Reinhold Niebuhr's sermon on humor, and that added to the list. The last struggle was with the issue of prayer. I had never felt comfortable with what I had learned in the church schools about prayer. I had tried to follow the instructions but always ended up with boredom and guilt.

I became aware that most of the parishioners I served in various congregations were bothered with the same problem. Most of them felt too guilty to say anything about it, which made their problem all the worse. The guilt-laden system of the church had made it difficult, if not impossible, for church members to wrestle honestly with their faith.

As is customary with ministers, much of this material has been worked out in sermons, and a great deal of credit goes to parishioners who helped me work it out. It came out of the crucible of my own experience, but my own experience, happily, has often also been the experience of those with whom I have worked.

In writing this book I had in mind people pretty much like myself. There are forces which draw one into the church and others which propel one out of it. Most of us within the church and on its fringes are acutely aware of the tension, and sometimes we just stick it out, feeling with Noah that the storm outside is a whale of a lot worse than the stink inside the ark. The book is written for those who love Jesus or maybe even want to love him and don't know how, and who are bothered by the inside of the ark and are always casting glances through the windows to see how the storm is doing.

The nearly final drafts of the manuscript were used for three study groups at Saint Luke's Presbyterian Church, Rolling Hills, California. They provoked a lot of discussion, some indignation, one letter of outrage, and a lot of fun. In other words, the groups were relatively successful.

This book represents a way station in my attempt to work out my "own salvation with fear and trembling," and I hope that it serves as an *agent provocateur* for someone else to do the same. It's a great struggle because it leads to freedom.

CHAPTER 1

THE DEBONAIRE DISCIPLE

He was a wanted man. The authorities were hunting for him on charges of murder and insurrection. Indeed, he had become so dangerous that even his comrades had turned against him. He fled into the wilds to escape the law. However, his exile was only an interlude in his revolutionary activities. After a crucial event during his flight he returned to lead a very successful revolt against the establishment. In his fight against the central government he poisoned the water supply, contaminated the sources of food, used various forms of biological warfare, and initiated a mass slaughter. He lured a heavily armed, mobile military strike force into a trap and destroyed it. All this he did with a ragtag passel of refugees who disputed his leadership and were poorly armed. One of his several biographers, in commenting on his lifetime of achievement, called him a "very meek" man, even more meek "than all men that were on the face of the earth."[1] His name was Moses.

Meekness is not an attribute that one would ordinarily associate with a political and religious revolutionary. But then again neither would one associate it with the queen of England. Several years ago, when Queen Elizabeth was being driven through the streets of Kingston, Jamaica, on one of her royal tours of the British Commonwealth, a gasp rose from the throng:

1. Num. 12:3.

"She meek." The seeming inappropriateness of the crowd's response lies in an ignorance of the Jamaican dialect, for among the country folk and townspeople of that island "meek" means making "an impression without fuss or posturing."[2]

Our modern problem with the word "meek" and with its application to figures like Moses and Elizabeth comes about because for us it implies submissiveness and servility. The way it is used in the Jamaican dialect comes much closer to the biblical usage. When the translators of the King James Version rendered the third beatitude, "Blessed are the meek, for they shall inherit the earth," they did not have in mind a tamed and spiritless person. For them the word bespoke an effortless, even regal, quality that showed no traces of striving. The meek were those who, like the queen and Moses, knew that their place before men was assured. Because they knew this through faith, they were not driven to prove themselves by posturing.

The French word for "meek" is *débonnaire,* which originally meant "of good race, breeding, or even nobility."[3] In modern times it has come to mean carefree, unruffled, and casually gracious—the personal qualities one would expect to find among the well-bred and aristocratic. The Greek word for "meek" had some of the same meanings. It was used to imply the idea of being tamed, not in the sense of being beaten into submission, but in the sense of being controlled and disciplined. It was used in this sense in the context of the training of athletes and fine horses. Also, it had the savor of the gentleness found among the high-minded

2. H. P. Jacobs, "Dialect, Magic and Religion," in *Ian Fleming Introduces Jamaica,* ed. Morris Cargill (London: Ándre Deutsch, 1965), p. 79.
3. R. Grandsaignes d'Hauterive, *Dictionaire d'Ancien Francais* (Paris: Librairie Larousse, 1947), p. 154.

and cultured.[4] Meekness, then, is not debasement. It is a disciplined gentility born of an inner confidence.

To the insecure this inner confidence often appears as arrogance, but it is at heart the product of trust, trust in one's own importance and place in life. As with Moses, it is a gift from God. Serenity is a threat to the unsure because it illuminates their inner disintegration. The confidence or inner trust of the debonaire disciple is the product of faith, of the fact that the meek think of life as a gift. The insecure think of it as an achievement. In classical Christian language the awareness of life as a gift has been called humility. However, that word is so overladen with a sense of humiliation that it has become almost useless today as a means of communication. The humility of the meek is not a dishrag and doormat mentality. It is an inner confidence rooted not in the self but in a trust in God's graciousness.

The standard American system of virtue has been based on an economy of achievement in which a person is encouraged to build up credits of worthiness through the things he does. This striving for achievement is, of course, grounded in an assumed and even encouraged sense of unworthiness. When a father tells his son to "go out and make something of yourself," the father is implying that the son is not worth much at the time. Guilt, a sense of unworthiness, and a feeling of inadequacy undergird a system of virtue that is rooted in achievement. The reason one seeks to prove himself is to counter the accusation that he is not up to snuff.

The confidence of the debonaire disciple is not a confidence in oneself based on how much one has

---

4. F. Hauck and S. Schulz, *"praus, prautēs,"* in *Theological Dictionary of the New Testament,* ed. Gerhard Kittel and Gerhard Friedrich, trans. Geoffrey W. Bromiley (Grand Rapids, Mich.: Wm. B. Eerdmans Publishing Co., 1964-), 6:646.

achieved but a confidence born of trust in the graciousness of God. It stands in stark contrast to that favored
American vice commonly called self-confidence which
really begins with self-rejection and which issues in a
ridiculous and destructive posturing produced by insecurity. It is debilitating advice to encourage a son to
strive for achievement on the basis of his adolescent
fears about his own worth and strength.[5]

The grace of the debonaire is seldom attributed to the
Christian in popular imagination. More often than not,
the Christian is seen as a dim, spiritless, lackluster personality or an aggressive moral boor. Christians are
people who carry the weight of the world on their shoul-
ders. Frequently, according to this popular image, there
is more than a slight tinge of masochism to their make-
up. They are people who have suffered and denied
themselves, and who seem to relish doing so. They are
spiritual bleeders, and one can always spot them by the
little red badge of humility they wear just over their
hearts. Or, if not spiritual bleeders, they are aggressive
types on the moral make. They are at pains to witness to
their own goodness and the sins of the world. In con-
tradistinction to our Lord's command they always let
their right hand know what their left hand is doing. They
are the classic American achievers, not in terms of
money, sex, or power, but in terms of goodness. But the
carefree quality of the debonaire has little in common
with either of these types of piety, for both of them are
after what the debonaire assume, a sense of significance.

In popular imagination the word "Christian" has fall-
en on hard times, along with the word "piety." Indeed, a
great deal of the time these words are used negatively.

---

5. William Barclay, ed., *The Gospel of Matthew*, 2 vols. (Philadelphia: Westminster Press, 1957–59), 1:92.

A pious person is either a mousy, timid soul or a moral bully and braggart. For many the Christian life is not a lively choice today. It would seem obvious to even the most casual observer, although the notion apparently has yet to dawn on many of the faithful, that freedom is better than captivity. Thus, the choices appear as either an outright rejection of Christianity in preference for some modern form of paganism with its totems and idols, or a continued submission to past "nonsense."

Piety is fundamentally a style of life, the way one lives. As such it involves the tone or quality of life as well as the particulars. It is formed by the fusion of three forces or dynamics that play upon every man. One is an estimate of the kind of world in which we live. Some would call it a happy garden and others a jungle. The way one lives depends in large measure upon what he thinks of the world he lives in. If a man thinks of his life as a perpetual struggle to survive, he will have a different feeling tone than if he thinks that all the institutions and organizations of modern culture are really concerned about the welfare of man.

The second force that goes into the making of a style of life is an estimate or assessment of the quality of man. Some would suggest that mankind is without any redeeming qualities at all, while others would argue that man is at heart good and that his evil is due only to ignorance and bad environment. Thus the first dynamic element of piety is concerned with social realities, the second with personal ones. One is a sociological assessment of society and the other a psychological assessment of the person.

The third force or element involved in piety is the question of the meaning of life, which is really a question about where one is heading, why one does things. In other words, what makes us run? A society based on achievement finds the meaning of life in getting ahead, in making a mark. In a militaristic society meaning hinges on one's ability to fit into a military system of conquest.

For the Christian, all three of these forces are bound up in Jesus Christ. In the cross of Christ the structures of society crucified God's graciousness. In the cross also is the paradox of man's malaise and God's grace. The cross reveals at one and the same time man's self-destruction and God's graciousness. The resurrection reveals God's power to overcome the sickness of both society and man.

Piety in the sense of a style of life is not only a Christian manifestation; it is a part of any cultural milieu. For instance, communism has its own version of piety, in which the realities of class conflict, the economic nature of man, and the eventual triumph of communism play a part. Marxism assumes that there is an essential and necessary conflict between the various classes of society, and this assumption then governs the citizen's response to the pressures of society. Since he believes that the proletariat will eventually triumph under the guise of communism, he gives himself to the promotion of conflict in order to hasten that triumph. Since he believes that the fundamental reality of man is economic, he sees everything in terms of money, property, and industry.

In contrast, modern capitalistic society has produced a piety in which competition, the demand to succeed, and the rewards of hard work are stressed in order to yield people who are fit for the system. Each culture develops a piety aimed at making its members function well in that culture. A capitalistic society demands an ever expanding economy, in contrast to a medieval system of barter, which requires a static means of exchange. The development of the energies necessary to produce such an economy requires a piety or style of life which places a premium on economic initiative. It does this best by creating a sense of insecurity which compels people to prove themselves acceptable in the society by their achievements.

On the other hand, the Christian faith at its best understands piety not so much in terms of fitting into the society but in terms of living both in it and above it. John speaks of living in the world without being of it, which produces a piety with the motif "one foot in heaven." This means that the other foot is planted squarely on the earth. It means living within a culture and yet not being trapped in it. As such it is not a useful piety which fits into the system, but it is a liberating piety which enables one to function well without being engulfed. The debonaire disciple is free from the burdens of coercion with which all societies try to fetter their members. He is free to live with life as a gift and not a burden.

A piety is not a fixed idea. Indeed, one of the chief problems confronting the development of a piety today is that many would hold onto life-styles of the past as if they were sacred. Such people wish to believe that a Christian style of life is the same for all generations and can be passed down from one generation to the next almost intact. The result is that piety becomes an arrested style of life, a relic of the past, a thing treasured in memory but not honored in practice.

Societies today are in constant change. Cultures are gradually, and sometimes cataclysmically, moving into new ways. Any piety or style of life which does not change with such rapidly changing times will be left behind, for a piety must be pertinent to a culture and to a person's place within it, without succumbing to that culture. The sad condition of piety today, for both the Protestant and the Roman Catholic, is an obvious illustration of this fact. The old modes of life are becoming less and less pertinent to the demands of contemporary life. A style congenial to small-town mid-America in the middle of the last century is hardly effective today in an industrialized, technological, and urban civilization—or barbarism, as you will. Yet although most of the customs of the traditional Protestant piety are really the province of social museums, much of modern Protestantism treats these museum pieces as if they were living realities and defends them as if they were the very gospel itself.

While there have been studies of past pieties and their inadequacy for today, very little, if anything, has been done to construct a piety that *is* pertinent for today. It has been pointed out that the Christian church in modern times has undergone two great theological revivals without a concomitant renewal among the faithful, but about all that has been done is to lament this state of affairs without doing some hard thinking about the reason for the lag.

Part of the problem has been the assumption of the perpetuity of old ways of life. Armed with this misapprehension, churchmen have tended either to discard the old piety as a relic of the past or constantly to reaffirm it in an act of mistaken devotion. Those who have discarded it spend their time deriding it with a supercilious sneer without offering an alternative to their rejection, as if to say that man does not need guides. Those who reaffirm the old pieties become in effect museum curators.

The breakdown of the traditional piety was caused by two things: its lack of a sound biblical orientation and the constant change in society. The flow of life makes the development of new forms of piety inevitable and worthwhile, but the weakness of the theological foundation of the traditional piety caused its adherents to buy the American assumption that one has to prove himself by achievement. This resulted in two classic forms of American religious outlook. One proved himself, on the one hand, by the degree of his humility. This produced the doormat believer, the "poor me" Christian whom few admire, especially the "poor-me's." On the other hand, one proved himself by his goodness. This produced the moral braggart who seemed bent on doing everyone in with his virtue.

The biblical mentality looks at the essence of life not in terms of achievement but in terms of relationship. The man who is bent on making the grade with God is an insufferable bore. But if a man sees his life as a gift and the heart of that gift as a relationship, then the tone of his life is gratitude. The former drives a man out to make himself a "success," while the latter gives a man the chance to respond to graciousness. The difficulty with the attitude of "making it" is that its roots are in despair. If a person is constantly trying to prove himself, the obvious implication is his own sense of unworthiness.

In times past the church has taught that the principal malady of man is his pride. The origins of that doctrine lay in the personal experiences of the men who framed the doctrine. They were men with large egos who had trouble with their spiritual extravagancies. The difficulty with the doctrine is that it leaves out the browbeaten little housewife who can hardly call her soul her own. While pride may be a sin, it is not the primal sin. It is merely a way of coping with that primal sin, a sense of unworthiness. One of the chief reasons that social organizations are able to coerce people so easily is that they correctly assume that people crave acceptance and approval. If any group can persuade the populace that its validation machine is better than someone else's, then they have built a better mousetrap, one that will catch a great many insecure mice. This form of madness is behind the appeal of social organizations which are based on snobbery, like country clubs, fraternities, and businessmen's clubs.

Men usually cope with their sense of unworthiness in one of two ways—either they relish it or they try to master it. In the church we have found two corresponding types of piety. On the one hand, there is the "humble," spiritless person who uses his sense of unworthiness as a tool to gain acceptance. This is the "poor little me" kind of piety which makes a virtue of being a doormat, and which has the vast power to coerce by means of pity. On the other hand, there is the supposedly self-assured person who by a kind of spiritual braggadocio attempts to intimidate everyone else with his own sacerdotal superiority. He is the aggressive Christian who is really a loudmouth posturing in the form of a moral bully. As different as these two types of piety appear, however, they have a common assumption, which is that a man must prove himself—the one by means of a cloying inferiority and the other by means of an outrageous superiority. Neither of them could be called debonaire, for they are both weighed down with the considerable burden of proof.

Also, the traditional piety has been largely individualistic and negative. A person made the grade mainly by what he did not do, rather than by what he did. This is an antivice morality. It ignores any kind of social issue beyond an immediate personal concern and sees its chief task as keeping to oneself. The result is a pure Christian unconcerned about the world around him, a Christian who is very unlike the carefree believer who is free to care about others.

Within the Christian community the attempt to prove one's own worthiness has taken three general forms, usually subtle and always devastating. For some such proof is to be found in the acceptability of one's ideas. A person has to think the right way. This approach has ranged all the way from the fundamentalists with their seemingly endless list of right doctrines to the avant-garde liberals who have fiercely insisted that their supposedly humane way of thinking is the only right way. There are few groups more insistent upon their own rectitude than the militant fundamentalists and the new left social activists. Both claim that there are right ideas and that there is no possibility of acceptance apart from acquiescence to these ideas. Doubts about doctrines and deviations from the party line are cause for ostracism. Thus the mind, which should be the means of gaining freedom, becomes a prison.

For others the means of winning acceptability lies in having the right emotions. Such "right" emotions run all the way from the conventional niceness and "deep feelings" of the discreet to the more flamboyant extravagancies of the cataclysmically converted. The one has that cozy holiness that comes from the spiritual lift of pleasant surroundings, and the other the emotional wrench of the tent meeting. Although these emotions may be genuine in themselves, they can become demonic and destructive when used as tests. If having a certain type of emotion becomes the criterion of acceptability, then what was once a free-flowing expression becomes a Procrustean bed in which everyone is cut down to size. There is, in fact, no such thing as a proper Christian feeling, and the attempt to force people into an emotional mold denies the peculiarity of people and the freedom of God to come and go as he wills.

For yet others right conduct has become the way to gain acceptability. Training in this attitude begins very early, when young people in the church are urged by large-bosomed, blue-haired ladies to be "nice little boys and girls." Now, of course, the niceness foisted on the young is really a means of controlling their behavior so that they will be more easily managed. The ethical principles of the biblical faith, which were originally designed to liberate men to become what God intended, have here become devices by which a group can intimidate others into a mold acceptable to it. But the Ten Commandments were given to man as guides and tutors, not as codes of restriction.

Because Christians pursued acceptability in the ways described, they came to be distinguished by a straitjacket quality of mind, sentimentalized emotions, and inhibited behavior. The object of the Christian life became the Christian and his improvement, in spite of Jesus' warning about saving one's own soul. This emphasis upon improvement was grounded in a false and contradictory view of man. According to this view, man is on the one hand completely unworthy, and yet on the other hand he is also responsible for his own improvement. In other words, this outlook was aimed at molding man by guilt into a better life. The function of the gospel was not to give man the assurance that he had already arrived in terms of God's love, but to point out and reinforce his unworthiness and to set rules by which he could better himself.

If one makes achievement and maturity the purpose of a style of life, then one must face the rot that takes place when a man feels that he has arrived. Ripeness is maturity, but ripeness is also a prelude to rot. If the great value is held to be in the striving and not in the arriving, then arrival is fundamentally unsatisfying. But life is more than a greyhound race with an artificial rabbit always just a few paces ahead. If a person denies this and adopts the piety of achievement, be it in terms of doctrines, emotions, or deeds, then he is left with the unenviable alternatives of the rot of maturity or the emptiness of never getting anyplace.

The classical Christian doctrine of man attempted to represent the ambiguity of life in the ideas of original sin and original righteousness. This doctrine held that man was originally created righteous but fell from that righteousness in an original sin. This meant that man was not created a sinful being; his sinfulness was rather a denial of his essential goodness. The traditional piety lost this classic sense of ambiguity by placing an exclusive emphasis upon man's sinfulness. The crucifixion was seen only in terms of man's unworthiness and almost never as God's loving affirmation of man. The impact of this piety was almost negative, and within this oppressive context it strove to improve people. It has not worked.

This negative attitude was, of course, at variance with the gospel, which is if anything an affirmation of life. If the assumption is made that man is essentially evil, then the enfleshment of God in Jesus Christ must be seen as an impossibility. The traditional piety was also contrary to the gospel in that it held that the decision always rests with man in the relationship between God and man. According to this inherited piety, the purpose of the Christian life was to make the grade with God, or if not with that transcendent a reality, at least with the church. In other words, it placed the initiative with man, not God, as can be seen in such sanctimonious semi-blasphemies as "making a decision for Christ," "finding Jesus," and "taking Jesus into our hearts." The Christian hope rests in the fact that in Christ God made a decision for man. There is no point in trying to find Jesus. He isn't lost. If anyone is looking for anyone else, it is Jesus who is looking for man. Finally, one does not take Jesus anywhere if he is indeed Lord of men. He is the one who takes man.

The negative character of the inherited piety can be seen in such plaintive and even whining hymns as

"What a Friend We Have in JESUS" and "Foul, I to the Fountain Fly." In contrast, there are such great hymns as "A Mighty Fortress Is Our God" and the modern "Lord of the Dance." In the former two hymns we are helped out of an essentially negative existence, while in the latter in the midst of our ambiguities we worship a God who is the source of our joy and life. In the former faith is an escape hatch from the perils and miseries of life, while in the latter the believer lives in the milieu of a faith in which God has conquered the forces that destroy man. The former is a retreat in the face of life; the latter is an affirmation in the context of uncertainty.

There has been a recent revival of this old style of piety under a new guise, in which the assumptions and structures remain largely the same. As this revival pales, an acute sense of the absence of a genuine piety becomes all the more apparent. The resurgence of the old piety has included the recent emphasis upon social action and concern. Like emotions, ideas, and ethics, these are not bad in themselves, but they become demonic when they are used to constrict life. Just as the death-of-God theology betrayed more than a trace of residual fundamentalism in its Jesus-only mentality, so the resurgent piety shows itself on closer inspection to be the child of its father.

The piety of social activism sees social action not as a manifestation and outpouring of faith but as a proof of it. The self-righteousness of the old piety remains and can be seen in the hostile rigidity of the social activists. Rather than proving their faith by not drinking or smoking, they try to do it by the correctness of their social dogmatism and by direct participation in acceptable social crises. But only certain social crises are acceptable. For instance, the elderly gradually being evicted from their homes by the government through unjust property taxation is not as acceptable as a riot in the ghetto, principally, one might suppose, because of the spectacular nature of the latter. This kind of piety might be called the piety of relevance.

The traditional piety and its modern version have common theological assumptions which contribute to the debility of both. They both assume that the Christian is something he does, rather than something he is. He proves himself a Christian either by avoiding certain things, as in the antivice morality, or by doing certain things, as in the social activist morality. The old piety would wonder endlessly whether or not a bartender could be a Christian, and the resurgent piety dismisses the racial bigot as a candidate for the faith. The system is the same; only the appearances have changed.

The doormat type of Christian piety has also found a more modern dress in what might be called the psychological maturity piety. Like the doormat variety, this is essentially a passive piety, in that it is not out breaking down the walls of wickedness but stays "within," repairing the outrages and wounds which life has inflicted on the soul. The mark of achievement for this psychological piety is maturity, and while maturity is seldom defined, it generally means being able to get along well in society without falling apart under pressure. This kind of piety views with disdain any unusual ideas or actions; the mature person is the ideal. The whole system ignores one salient reality, however, which is that maturity is a prelude to death. Adolescent behavior is viewed as unacceptable, it being forgotten that adolescence is at least a time of growth. The piety of maturity wants to get off the high seas of growth and turbulence into the port of emotional mellowness.

Unlike those who adhere to these other forms of piety, the debonaire disciple is not trying to get anywhere, for he has already arrived. The hint of nobility found in the meekness of the third beatitude is to the point, for the debonaire disciple, like the nobleman, no longer has to prove himself. Being carefree, he can afford to be careful. There is a sense of frenetic desperation found in many of the old pieties and their more modern forms. If the gentleness of nobility comes from belonging to a noble line of succession, then the gentleness of the Christian comes from belonging to an even more noble line of succession. As Paul would say, if we are children of God, then we are heirs, "heirs of God and fellow heirs with Christ" (Rom. 8:17).

The Christian begins with the assurance of God's graciousness. Authentic biblical piety begins where other systems of piety hope to get. The Christian life is an expression of one's security in God's love, not a claim upon it on the basis of having proven oneself. The debonaire disciple lives a responsive life, responsive to the graciousness of God in Christ. Because of this he is not terrified by the moral ambiguity of his own life, dismayed by the uncertainties of his mind, or disturbed by the turbulence of his emotions. In other words, he is not paralyzed into inaction or driven into illusory behavior by his fear of being wrong. He is free to live, think, feel, and act in a confusing, absurd, and baffling world. He is free genuinely to care, not about himself but about the whole of God's creation around him.

The dynamics of the piety of the debonaire disciple result in his assessment of the society in which he finds himself and his own understanding of himself under the aspect of God's grace. He can afford to live fully and freely in this world because he lives *sub specie aeternitatis,* under the aspect of the eternity of God's love in Jesus Christ.

CHAPTER 2

THE METAPHYSICS OF PIETY

Piety is a style of life, the way one lives. It is a matter of the tone of one's behavior as well as the behavior itself. The construction of a style of life, like all constructive efforts, necessitates paying close attention to the dynamics of structures. If someone chooses to play baseball, he must heed the rules of the game. If a person builds a sailboat, he must be aware of the interplay of wind and water. Piety is no different. One must attend to the winds of the Spirit as well as to the waters of one's particular pond.

In the Gospel of Matthew, our Lord instructs his disciples about the wind and water of their lives as he sends them out on their first mission. He advises them: "Behold, I send you out as sheep in the midst of wolves; so be wise as serpents and innocent as doves" (10:16). This advice is about the dynamics of a functioning piety. Jesus offers an assessment of the world in which man lives: it is the world of the wolves. He suggests an estimate of human life when he speaks of a reptilian wisdom and a dovelike integrity. Finally, he speaks of life itself as a journey, a pilgrimage in which man is always going out into places he has never been.

The metaphysics of piety is concerned with these fundamental dynamics, for metaphysics is the type of thinking that looks beyond appearances to realities. What is really going on? is a metaphysical question which every intelligent person should ask, though a great many people today remain content with images and fronts. In this they are less metaphysicians than is the child who drives his parents wild with his perennial question, "But why?" An inquisitive frame of mind, a restlessness with appearances, and a questioning of claims are the qualities of a metaphysician.

Every type of society or civilization has a style of life, or a piety, on which it places a premium. As we noted earlier, in a capitalistic society the honors go to the so-called successful man, for the elementary reason that it takes successful men to make the system work. The assumptions behind this piety of success are accepted by its advocates as unquestionable truths. The world is seen as fundamentally competitive; the belief is firmly held that without competition nothing worthwhile will ever get done. The meaning of life is to be found in achievement and success, and man's fundamental meaning lies in gaining the approval of the system through what he accomplishes.

Christian piety stands in direct contrast to this piety of success. Its first element is the realization that life is a journey, not a destination. Jesus sent his disciples out; they were not to "arrive." Secondly, the world is viewed as the province of wolves. Jesus cautioned his disciples to beware of men (Matt. 10:17). In other words, he thought that the world was hostile to the welfare of man. This is no sanguine optimism, but rather an almost chilling realism which can be tolerated and understood only if it is accepted as a preliminary assessment and not an ultimate one. Finally, the estimate of man of Christian piety is that of the gospel. Man's meaning and integrity come neither by his achievements nor by his submission, but by his faith. Jesus uses two distinctive words — "sheep" and "dove" — both of which are symbols in biblical imagery for those to whom God has

given his love. In other words, within the biblical understanding man does not achieve status but receives it as a
gift.

As has been pointed out, there can be no one piety
which is valid for all time, for styles of life must change
from one age to the next and from one civilization to the
next. Yet although there can be no fixed life-style there
is a metaphysics of piety which really represents the
fundamental dynamics of the Christian faith. There are
basic questions which must be asked of any piety, questions about its authenticity and integrity.

Any piety which claims to be Christian and at the
same time operates with a sanguine view of society is
simply without integrity. The wolves of the world will
always wear the clothing of sheep, and although that
clothing may change in fashion, the wolflike quality of
life will not change. The symbols may vary, but the
reality remains constant. Likewise, if a piety claims to
be Christian and still stresses achievement as a means of
integrity, a profound compromise has been made which
throws the authenticity of that piety into question.
Again, the symbols of achievement may vary from time
to time and group to group, but the reality of achievement remains hostile to the Christian faith. A man driv-
en to excel in order to prove himself is a far cry from a
man excelling because he enjoys his life. A student
grinding away in the library to make the grades is not
the same thing as a student pursuing knowledge because
he finds it rewarding.

Each version of piety has its own metaphysics, its
own dynamics. The Christian begins with the radical
assertion of the basic graciousness of life in Jesus
Christ, the alienation and hostility of the world in which
we live, and the expeditionary quality of life. In the
relationship between God and man the initiative is with

God, which is to say that man does not need to prove himself before God. Rather, God comes to man graciously to accept and redeem him. The Christian's life is a response to God's love, not a series of achievements aimed at earning that love.

In addition to a sense of responsiveness about life, the Christian also has a deep sense of its moral ambiguity. The traditional pieties, both religious and secular, have never really come to terms with the reality of this ambiguity. The religious ones were at once both excessively pessimistic about man and excessively optimistic in the expectation that one so bad could become good. They thought that by an act of the will the evil of man could be changed to virtue. The secular pieties were seldom aware of the pervasive moral malaise of man. Those who espoused the capitalistic ethic of achievement seldom saw the moral and spiritual ruin that this ethic causes. The constant drive to produce and achieve may accomplish a great deal, but the price paid in terms of driven and compulsive men, lonely women, and children raised in a pressure-cooker atmosphere is a frightful price to pay for things that could be gained another way.

An authentic piety assumes a moral ambiguity. In addition to the original sin of the traditional piety, it also assumes an original righteousness. In the story of the fall in the third chapter of Genesis, man is not created evil. He becomes evil as a result of his own decision. In assessing one's situation in this world, there is a temptation to make one of two naive decisions. One is to regard the world as a basically good place in which the evil is merely a mistake or the result of lack of knowledge. The other is to regard it as an essentially evil place in which the good is merely a fleeting aberration. Both deny the real ambiguity that confronts most of us. The good we experience is really an admixture of good and evil, and the evil we experience is often the result of the best of intentions.

If one faces up to the real ambiguity, the grayness of life, then one must make another decision about the quality of that grayness. Is it black tinged with occasional touches of white, or is it white sullied by black? Is disloyalty a negation of loyalty, or is loyalty an oddity in a world of disloyalty? Is truth a fiction, or is a lie the denial of truth?

God did not make an evil world, but a good one, and the evil in it is the negation by man of that goodness. Goodness rests upon freedom, for a good act coerced is not really a good act. A constrained loyalty is not a real loyalty, but a submission. In making the world good, God also made it free, which is to say that he created in goodness the possibility of evil. This is the terror of Christian freedom. The awful consequences of such a creation can only be borne in an aura of grace.

The negative quality of evil in no way diminishes its forbidding force. Seeing disloyalty as a negation of loyalty in no way reduces the force of the disloyalty. Rather, it is seeing evil for what it is—a destruction of the goodness of God's creation. When our Lord sent the disciples out as sheep in the midst of wolves, he was sending them out into a destructive world. The cross as one of the chief symbols of the Christian faith bears visible testimony to this terribly ambiguous world. Roman law and Jewish religion, the two finest products of the human society of the time, conspired to destroy the graciousness of God under the aegis of goodness. The cross stands both for human wickedness and for God's mercy. In the cross man was at once in need of mercy and apparently in God's eyes worth it.

The need of man to be right, good, or true is an indication of his pervasive insecurity. His difficulty in accepting the provisional quality of life has been the source of most of the tyrannies to which he has sub-jected himself. In this most ambiguous of all possible worlds he has attempted to rid himself of his feeling of insecurity by fastening himself down with the stakes of dogmatism and moralism. He has had a compulsive need to be right when in fact he could never be sure. Man is a pilgrim, and once he reaches port, his journey, like his life, is finished. This is to say that man lives by faith, not by knowledge. The most important things in which he believes cannot be established.

The traditional piety broke down because of its irrele-vance to modern society, and also because of its repres-sive character. Any attempt to escape the awful in-security of freedom by clinging to some form of certainty always involves a repression. In effect, it is an attempt to make ultimate things that are really relative. If a man claims to live by his goodness, he must ignore the moral ambiguity of his own life. He fashions his own fetters, thinking that he has gained meaning when in fact he has merely inhibited himself. The futile anger of many of the social activists is an indication of their insecurity, for once a dogmatism or a principle has been sanctified, it can no longer be questioned. If it is ques-tioned, then the supposed security is threatened, bring-ing about further repression and hostility.

A style of life which is negative and repressive may have great initial force, but in the long run it is destruc-tive and finally wears itself out. Guilt may be used once in a while, like abuse, but as a style of life for a lifetime it finally breeds a bitter and hostile personality. A piety rooted in negation cannot be the source of creativity. Rage as a basic response to life is ravaging.

If a man does not hate at certain times, there is something amiss. If a person is not enraged at injustice, there is something wrong with his humanity, but if his style is rage, there is something even greater wrong with his humanity. Rage as a style, hostility as a piety, are ruinous, but as responses to given events they can be a basic affirmation of life. A man without anger is a man without values, but an angry man is a man destroying his own values.

The greatest weakness of the traditional piety was its theological inadequacy. Indeed, it was a profound corruption of the Christian faith. In its compulsion to look at life as an achievement rather than as a gift, it destroyed man's capacity to enjoy his life. In much of the traditional piety, enjoyment was viewed with disfavor. Since the style of this piety was guilt, enjoyment was a threat. The suppressed rage found in much of the old piety and in its newer forms is a vivid testimony to its lack of grace.

The traditional piety was unable to come to terms with the ambiguity of life. To cope with the feeling of insecurity it built fortresses of security which, when they came under attack, made the insecurity all the worse. Each new insecurity merely caused intensified efforts at security. This piety was in no sense a liberation. It was hardly debonaire. It was a denial of the gospel.

If life is a pilgrimage rather than a destination, then all of man's beliefs and assertions have a provisional quality to them. Our Lord's advice to his disciples is particularly pertinent here. He enjoins them to have the wisdom of the serpent and the innocence of the dove. Innocence in this context is not the nonsense of being without stain. It is the integrity which comes as the gift of love. In the end a man thinks well of himself because someone has loved him well. This begins as a small child and extends throughout his life to his death. If he thinks that God has loved him in Jesus Christ, then this is his ultimate integrity. It is the gift of God's graciousness.

The authenticity which comes as a gift enables a man to look at life with a certain serpentine savvy. He is not about to be taken in. It is a savvy not only about the pretensions of those around him but also about his own pretensions. One might say that a biblical piety is characterized by its lack of commitments. Real religion cannot begin until a man is disillusioned not only about everyone else but also about himself.

This sense of the provisional turns the customary Protestant pieties upside down. It entails living by questions rather than by answers. Skepticism, not credulity, may be the mark of an authentic faith in an ambiguous world. A lack of commitment may be the mark of a heartfelt response to graciousness, rather than commitment. A sense of humor may have more integrity in dealing with all the nonsense of life than the customary solemnity that passes as an exhibition of Christian faith.

The drive to find answers rather than to live with questions often results in a rationalism in which all the answers have supposedly been found. But an ambiguous world is also an absurd one. Most things do not fit, and the attempt to make them fit ignores the root absurdity of life. Having the answers has little place in a world in which life changes so fast that most people are giving answers to yesterday's questions, not having quite realized what questions are being asked today.

The metaphysics of Christian piety includes these three fundamental elements: a sense that life is a pilgrimage and not a destination; an understanding of the pervasive moral malaise and ambiguity of life; and finally, a belief that life is a gift from God. Thus life is not an achievement, but a response to God's graciousness in Jesus Christ. Its motif is gratitude, not acquisition. The Christian is free from the baggage of rectitude and proof. He is free to be carefree without being careless, because his assurance is not rooted in the moral ambiguity of achievement, but in God's gracious disposition toward man. He has the freedom of the well-born, those who have been born anew in faith.

CHAPTER 3

THE REMEMBRANCE OF
THINGS PAST

There had been a mutiny aboard one of the ships of the Royal Navy. British marines from the flagship, H.M.S. *Duke of Cumberland,* had boarded the H.M.S. *Ulysses* to subdue the mutineers by force, with heavy casualties. Indeed, the situation had become so grave that the first sea lord of the admiralty had seen fit to dispatch Vice-Admiral Vincent Starr, assistant director of naval operations, from his vital post in London north to Scapa Flow in the Orkney Islands off the coast of Scotland, with broad powers to investigate and resolve the crisis.

Starr accused commissioned officers of His Majesty's navy of sympathy with the mutiny in the ranks. In response Surgeon Commander Brooks of the *Ulysses* said that the conditions prevailing on the North Sea run to Murmansk were so unremittingly cruel and harsh that the customary rules of discipline were no longer adequate.

"Mankind, of course, can and does adapt itself to new conditions. Biologically and physically, they have had to do so down through the ages, in order to survive. But it takes time, gentlemen, a great deal of time. You can't compress the natural changes of twenty centuries into a couple of years; neither mind nor body can stand it. You can try, of course, and such is the fantastic resilience and toughness of man that he can stand it—for extremely short periods. But the limit, the saturation capacity is soon reached. Push men beyond that limit and anything can happen. I say 'anything' advisedly, because we don't yet know the precise form the crack-up will take — but crack-up there always is."[1]

The story is fictional, its setting the period of the Second World War. While it may be fictional, however, its diagnosis and prognosis of man are not. What Surgeon Commander Brooks spoke of we now call "future shock." The way we respond to it is with the remembrance of things past. A man draws strength to face the challenges of the present and the anticipation of the future from the reservoir of his memory. The charts and maps sailors use to cross the seas are in fact the transcribed memories of previous voyages, and if an adventurer sails into uncharted seas, the wits that bring him through are tutored by his past experiences. An inexperienced man on an unknown journey is all the more endangered by his lack of memory. Modern man facing the turbulence of today and the uncharted seas of tomorrow stands in grave need of a memory to give him the perspective not only to endure but also to prevail.

Change is a form of death, for like death it entails a loss. Even though one may not lament the loss, one is still forced to adapt to a different constellation of experiences. Upon liberation, people who have endured the horrors of concentration camps speak of the loss of deep friendships made while imprisoned. They find that it takes time to adjust to the very conditions for which they had longed. Even the worst of circumstances is not without some redeeming goodness, and so when one is freed from what he detests, he feels the loss of those things that made his hardship bearable.

1. Alistair MacLean, *H.M.S. Ulysses* (Greenwich, Conn.: Fawcett Publications, 1955), p. 27.

Change is even worse for those who lament what is lost, for with the loss they have been deprived of something treasured, something that gave life substance and meaning. Heirlooms sold, trinkets misplaced, jobs automated, fashions altered, landmarks forgotten — all can be small forms of death. The tides of history have a way of eroding those things which most men hold dear.

As Surgeon Commander Brooks pointed out, most men can adapt to varied circumstances. The unique problem facing modern man, however, is the overwhelming nature of the change. It comes on with the force of a battleship; it is incessant and offers no respite. There appears to be no way to resist it or recuperate from it. One feels like a mere victim of the vicissitudes of life.

Nearly everyone marvels at the capacity of Rose Kennedy to sustain herself during a series of family tragedies any one of which would do in most mortals. In some ways the Kennedy family stands out as a paradigm of the pains of modernity. They have had to bear incessant grief and remain intact. Modern man has had to bear incessant change and not cave in. There should be little wonder that modern Western man is a psychic mess and that his children are bizarre. The process of grief takes time, and the unrelenting change of the modern era has left precious little time for such repair and recuperation.

In addition to being a sense of loss, grief is also a feeling of guilt over the past and a foreboding about the future. A widow must cope with not only her personal loss but also her guilt feelings and her fears of the future, which is obscure. Change thus involves a fear of the future as well as a loss of the past. Often one's psychic energies are exhausted just in adjusting to the loss, without the additional burden of facing the morrow.

Surgeon Commander Brooks predicted that men would crack up under the pressure of the constant grief of adaptation to rapid and incessant change. One can see this crack-up taking place in modern society. The frenetic quality of life is but the tip of the iceberg of a deeper despair over the loss of values in a society in the process of disintegration.

There are several widespread responses to the stress of this crack-up. One is the desire to forget or ignore what is happening. The pursuit of pleasure and entertainment among the affluent is not much different emotionally from the adolescent cop-out by means of narcotics. Both are responses to overwhelming pressure and means of escape. Another way people try to cope with the grief of future shock is with the device of nostalgia. Oddly enough, this nostalgia is not confined to those who can recollect cherished past events. The frontier garb of the drugstore cowboy, the granny glasses of the female adolescent, and the return to the rustic life in the communes are all examples of a desire either to create an instant tradition or to flee to a past never known. Everyone lapses into nostalgia on occasion, but as a style of life it is a flight. Unlike memory, it is not a recollection of significant events of the past to aid one in living in the present and anticipating the future. Rather, it is a denial of the present and a retreat from the future by an attempted return to something that no longer exists, so that one will not have to cope at all.

An example of nostalgia is the contemporary idealization of the Civil War. The middle-aged men who tramp around wearing "authentic reproductions" of old uniforms have little understanding of that conflict and its meaning for the present. Unlike this nostalgic escape through playacting, a true sense of history is a means of understanding the dynamics of the present and a way to anticipate the structures of the future. Lincoln showed such a sense of history in his second inaugural address when he tried to understand what had happened to the nation, why the conflict had come, and how to face the future. He suggested that American slavery was an offense which God had allowed to continue through his appointed time but now willed to remove, and that the war was "the woe due to those by whom the offense came." He continued by speaking of the future: "With malice towards none; with charity for all; with firmness in the right, as God gives us to see the right, let us strive on to finish the work we are in; to bind up the nation's wounds; to care for him who shall have borne the battle, and for his widow, and for his orphan—to do all which may achieve and cherish a just, and a lasting peace, among ourselves, and with all nations."[2]

Lincoln was trying to understand what had happened so that he could manage the present and plan for the future. The better a nation comprehends its past, the better it can cope with the present and anticipate the future. The American dream of freedom for all men and the history of slavery must be appreciated to understand the present turmoil of the country, and the degree of bigotry one finds in the American consciousness will certainly affect one's estimation of the future. The future may be a surprise, but it does not have to be so great a shock.

If a person has no remembrance of things past to give him the ability to cope with the present and anticipate the future, then his only escape is the nihilism of oblivion. The busyness and frenzy of the affluent classes and the torpor of the addicts are both forms of living outside of life because there is no sense of the past. The nostal-

2. Abraham Lincoln, *The Collected Works of Abraham Lincoln,* ed. Roy P. Basler, vol. 8 (New Brunswick, N.J.: Rutgers University Press, 1955), p. 333.

gic find themselves re-creating a false past that holds neither threats nor promises, only ease, a disease of escape.

In the modern "age of discontinuity" man is tempted to live without the remembrance of his past. He becomes so dazzled by his achievements that he makes the mistake of thinking that they invalidate the meaning of the past, when in fact their foundations were laid in that past. A young man without a father always has difficulty defining himself as a man because he has no point of reference. Even in rebellion against his father a young man is working out his meaning in reference to his history. He may accept it or reject it, but it stands there as a point of reference and an aid to understanding. A young man without a father is a man without a point of reference, and a civilization without a sense of history is one which cannot understand itself, much less apprehend its future.

There is a tragic irony in a man who can see more clearly than did his father and yet stands at his father's shoulder condemning him for his blindness. One may know more than those who went before, but that increased knowledge is no wisdom if it does not encompass the realization of one's own blind spots and insights as well as those of one's predecessors. Man is a historical animal, and without a remembrance of things past he has neither capacities for the present nor the ability to anticipate the future.

Many people resent and resist the idea of tradition, thinking that it somehow binds them to a repetition of the past. But without a knowledge of one's history the possibility is greater that one will be condemned to such a repetition. In other words, one cannot learn without a remembrance of things past, for in fact the sum of man's knowledge is really his history. Knowledge is not merely the gathering of facts and experiences, it is also the grasp of their meaning, and for this time is required. If we live in an era of future shock, our memories can be shock absorbers. They can give us the perspective by which we can live amidst turmoil.

Memory is not merely a recollection of past events, for it includes an understanding of their meaning, a way of looking at them. Just as history is not merely chronology, so memory is not merely recital. The communal memories that surface at the funeral of a loved one are not simply an enumeration of previous incidents, for they are laden with the meaning of the love given and received within that family. The acts of sacrifice remembered at the death of a mother or father are not simply events recited, for they are symbols of how the bereaved looks at himself in the present. The gift of love in the context of sacrifice is one of those points of reference and identity that give understanding of the present and the ability to anticipate the future. The sense that one has been loved well helps one grasp the immediate and look to the events yet to come. When everything seems out of kilter, the balance given by memory is not just an option, it is a necessity.

In an age of discontinuity a man cannot live well nor indeed long without a memory, for if he is to endure the grief of change and prevail over the fright of an unknown future, then he must possess a memory laden with meaning, a perspective on life. Tradition is a form of communal memory. The traditions of a nation are the communal memories which form the basis of its meaning. The holocaust of the Civil War is part of the tradition or communal memory of America, and without the remembrance of that past the nation is without an adequate understanding of itself.

The rebellion of the blacks in America today is a radical threat to anyone unfamiliar with the promises of freedom and the realities of slavery in the American past. It seems like a discontinuity because the blacks had been outwardly servile. With the advent of the civil rights movement this has changed, and both whites and blacks have had to adjust to a new mode of relationship. Both have had to search their communal memories for some understanding of the apparent discontinuities that overwhelm them. The incoherence of much of the talk today about the black quest for justice, on the part of both blacks and whites, is an effect of future shock. Man needs the shock absorber of his memory to deal with such effects.

Memory, then, is more than a recital of the facts of history. It also involves the way one interprets these facts, which depends on where one stands in faith. The American Revolution was either an insurrection among the provincials or a War of Independence, depending on one's attitude. Likewise, the crucifixion was either the execution of an itinerant part-time rabbi and carpenter, or it was God in his love for man personally suffering for the sins of the world; how one looks at it depends on where one stands in faith. Memory, then, is a perspective on life in which one reads the meaning of the past through faith in order to cope and conquer. This perspective in turn affects one's understanding of the present and determines whether one's attitude toward the future is one of foreboding or anticipation.

The capacity of man to adapt, adjust, and prevail in the chaos of change in an age of discontinuity rests in his awareness of his heritage. A man's sense of tradition is always a matter of adoption and confirmation. Even though he may be born into a community with a strong sense of tradition, he must still appropriate that tradition for himself. Also, he may move in as a stranger and adopt a new tradition. An immigrant from Europe, if he chooses to be an American, must finally adopt George

Washington as the father of his country and must see Abraham Lincoln as the Great Emancipator. Paul speaks of God adopting believers as sons, which means that they can then think of Abraham as their father. In other words, the debonaire disciple is the inheritor of a great tradition which found its culmination in Jesus Christ. As the word "meek" would indicate, he has a certain ancestral nobility, his ancestor being Jesus Christ, the Son of God.

Peter Drucker has pointed out that within the past decade, industry and technology have changed so much that much of the past understanding of economic dynamics may be irrelevant for a grasp of the present and an anticipation of the future. Our technological society has been built upon structures developed during the first decade of this century, and understanding of those structures has served us very well up to this point.[3] However, we are now in a new era.

Drucker may be right with his "new era" theory of civilization, especially if his thesis is confined to technological matters, but as anyone who reads anything of the past knows, man is constantly being subjected to a "new era" critique of his troubles. The eighteenth century fondly called itself the age of the Enlightenment and everything that went before it the Dark Ages. It saw a discontinuity. We speak about discontinuity as if to say that each civilization is somehow a self-contained unit, hermetically sealed from the contaminants of previous civilizations. But the ages of Greece and Rome were not separate and discrete units. The United States before and after the Civil War was still the same country. There was a change, and a profound one, but that change cannot be understood apart from what went before it.

3. Peter Drucker, *The Age of Discontinuity* (New York and Evanston: Harper and Row, 1968), pp. 3 ff.

Drucker's point is well taken if he means to say that some ways of understanding lose their force and vitality with the passage of time. The manner in which a mother adjusts to and copes with a helpless infant is surely not appropriate when that child has become a burgeoning adolescent. Her memory should have a greater span, her grasp of the realities of life a greater range and depth. If she fails to transcend particulars in her memory, then she ceases to adapt well and sometimes lapses into nostalgia about "those wonderful years when Johnny was such a sweet baby," blotting out the unpleasantness of the past in her eagerness to escape that of the present. Such escapism is harmful to both her and her child.

Memory must have more depth than a simple nostalgia which forgets the pains and inconveniences, for these are a vital part of events and their interpretation. One possibly learns more from the pains of the past than from the pleasures. Nostalgia is a denial that suffering can be redemptive. In other words, if memory is really going to serve us well in understanding the present and anticipating the future, it must be informed by a profound understanding of human nature and the dynamics of history. Lincoln had learned from the pain of the Civil War; he possessed a profound grasp of man and history.

If an exceptionally successful man understands himself in the present solely on the premise that he deserves everything he has because he has worked for everything he has, then his grasp of his personal history is simply not profound. It is a shallow tit-for-tat view of life which can in no way cope with the absurd and random events that overtake every man. For instance, it has not the slightest capacity to cope with death, which cannot be escaped by hard work. But worse than that, it eliminates from the picture the apparently fortuitous events that are in fact the ingredients of success just as much as hard work is. Being at the right place at the right time is not the result of some capitalistic virtue. Depending upon one's stance it is either blind luck or providence, but in no case is it the issue of goodness.

The debonaire disciple is one whose memory is informed by the contours of the biblical faith. He understands his past not merely in terms of some tribal or nationalistic deity, or the vagaries of chance, or some private totem whose existence depends on his pleasure. The principal ingredient of a biblical memory is the grasping of history as a drama in which the turmoil of the present, the disorders of the past, and the apprehensions of the future are all seen in the light of the end.

Most modern men have structured their memories in one of two ways, which could be represented by the squirrel cage and the escalator. Some think that life is an endless series of repetitions without any conclusion or end. Today is a repetition of yesterday and a rehearsal for tomorrow. One has the feeling of not going anywhere. This is essentially an enervating and pessimistic outlook on life. It is a "squirrel cage" from which there is no escape. There was a World War I and a World War II, and there will be a World War III.

Others think of life as a gradual movement upward. The inevitable course of history is one of improvement. Things are getting better day by day, or at least age by age. Just as the age of the Enlightenment called the time before it the Dark Ages, with the obvious implication of improvement, so many contemporaries look at previous ages or even generations as preliminary or inferior. This view has some obvious disadvantages. It blinds one to the genius of the past. It is adolescently arrogant. It encourages a love of the new for the sake of the new. Worst of all, it does not even have the modest advantage of squaring with the facts. One doubts that anything in the Middle Ages could really compare with the horrors of Nazi Germany. The terrors of the twentieth century simply do not fit with the notion that modern man is an improvement over ancient man.

The squirrel-cage theory of memory is destructively enervating. The escalator theory of memory lays the foundation for arrogant illusions. Neither really gives an adequate and hopeful understanding of the flow of life. A possible modification combines the two into a theory of memory in which the repetitions of the squirrel cage are transmuted into revolutions of improvement. However, this theory also suffers from arrogance. It assumes that although there are ups and downs in history, there is still a gradual although imperceptible improvement.

A sense of direction is essential for life. One must have the feeling of going somewhere. But the escalator understanding of history makes the mistake of thinking that a sense of direction assumes an improvement. The traditional Christian understanding of memory does not make that fatal assumption. Rather than seeing life as a "squirrel cage" or an "escalator," it uses the images of a pilgrimage or journey and a drama. There is a sense of direction and purpose, but it is not burdened with the illusions of adolescence.

In every drama there occurs a crisis point at which the conclusion becomes foregone. In a war there is always a battle in which the tide of the war changes and the outcome becomes evident. Such an event was the advent of Jesus Christ, in which the times and tides of men were changed and the conclusion of history was made known. Even in the midst of apparent defeat and failure, the debonaire disciple has the sense that he is still going somewhere.

Archbishop William Temple once said that the fruit of the Christian faith is the ability to see life steadily and to see it whole. This posture is quite a contrast to the

frenzy of modern society, which is a yielding to neo-
philia, the love of the new, which is in turn a repudiation
of the past. If all that a man has to live by is his
immediate context, then he becomes a victim of his
sensations. The new is all that he has. The frenzy is also
a yielding to the enervating pessimism of the squirrel
cage. If a man is not going anywhere, he is tempted to
indulge himself in the fancies of the new. He has no
protection against the "psychic epidemics" that seem to
sweep modern culture.

The neophiliac sometimes has the appearance of the
debonaire, but he is actually careless rather than carefree. The shock of the future has become too much for
him. He cannot adapt fast enough, and as a consequence
he either runs away or embraces the new without a
sense of discrimination. The cares become too great,
and therefore he becomes careless, rather than carefree.
The neophiliac is "being carried rapidly forward into
some nebulously 'modernistic' future,"[4] but he has no
control and no sense of destiny. He falls victim to psychic epidemics because he has no memory.

In Jesus Christ, God assumed the human situation
and subjected himself to all the terrors, rigors, and pleasures of man. He endured the cross and prevailed in the
resurrection. God has been where man is and won. This
was the decisive turning point in the history of man, and
it augurs his destiny. A biblical memory is fundamental
for the debonaire disciple, because it gives him the capacity to see life steadily and to see it whole. It immu-
nizes him from the psychic epidemics of the modern era.
It allows him to be carefree without being careless, so
that he finally can be careful. Most men spend their lives
finding out where they are going. The debonaire disciple

4. Christopher Booker, *The Neophiliacs* (London: Collins, 1969), p.
36.

begins where other men hope to get, for they go out seeking to justify their lives by their accomplishments while he begins with a justification by faith. Like a true aristocrat, he has a sense of destiny without a compulsion to arrive. In addition to understanding himself under the aspect of God's steadfast love and loyalty, he senses his destiny, the intimation of which he has seen in Jesus Christ.

During the agonies of the Battle of the Bulge and the terrors of Iwo Jima, the American nation moved with a sense of destiny. The awfulness of those battles was made bearable by an act of faith which saw the end as victory. In contrast there was the stark loneliness of the Nazi concentration camp, where men had been cut off from all hope. They gave up because they could see nothing to get them through to the future. In this they could serve as a ghastly paradigm of our civilization. Cut off from his past, denied his future, modern man has given up. The despair of the concentration camp inhabitants was agony; the quiet despair of the neophiliac, while far less noble, is no less a slide into death.

The future shock of modern civilization is made bearable by the shock absorber of a biblical memory; it is finally conquered by the hope rooted in that memory. Hope is a special quality of the debonaire disciple; it is not the same thing as wishful thinking. Like nostalgia wishful thinking represents a desire to escape, only it projects reveries into the future instead of the past. Anticipation of the future and understanding of the present are rooted in the remembrance of things past. Love of the present and hope for the future are grounded in a faith born of a biblical memory, a memory infused with the actions of God in Jesus Christ, in which he endured and prevailed.

CHAPTER 4

MEN OF LITTLE FAITH

Two broken-down actors are employed by a circus. They could not even be classed as has-beens, because they never really were. One is a cynical, angry young man, the other a pompous old man. Enduring the cold blasts of their adversity, they try to warm themselves emotionally, but they are unable even to recall the glow of past glories. Instead, they build the flimsy shelters of cynicism and pomposity to shield themselves from their chilling circumstances. Nickles, the younger man, has been reduced to selling popcorn; Mr. Zuss, the older man, sells balloons.

As they walk about the empty circus tent, they are caught up in an ancient drama, the story of Job. The young cynic takes the role of Satan, the old windbag that of God. While they are feeling out their roles, Nickles tells Mr. Zuss that he will need a mask to play God. Mr. Zuss expresses surprise and sarcastically asks where he could find a mask of God. Nickles bitterly refers him to heaven, which he calls the great lost-and-found, and says:

> If God should laugh
> The mare would calf . . .
> The cow would foal. . . .
> Diddle my soul.

Mr. Zuss screams in reply, "God never laughs! In the whole Bible!" Nickles bitterly retorts:

How could he laugh? He made it —
              the toy
Top — the world — the dirty whirler![1]

Laughter and piety, humor and faith, seldom go hand in hand for the modern mind. The believer is pictured as a humorless drone. Hilarity and worship are inappropriate in the same phrase. The life of faith for most is without gaiety.

Gravity and solemnity are the hallmarks of a man of faith in the popular imagination, and they are also signs of modern civilization. While we may hear a great deal of laughter today, its vibrations are too brittle and nervous to gladden the heart. More often than not, they are the expression of despair and cynicism. Modern man is above all the product of a rational civilization. He does not believe in mystery, for he thinks that it will finally yield to the canons and strictures of logic. All the unknowns can be known, all the mysteries solved, all the absurdities made reasonable.

Up to the eighteenth century man still had a Gothic mind. He believed that there were dark terrors of the night, unseen forces of destruction that could rend a man unawares. It was an ambiguous world, shadowy and dark, in which the brilliance of reason illuminated only heavenly things and eternal verities.

With the eighteenth century reason and nature were joined. The highest expression of logic, mathematics, was applied to the dumb, brute forces of nature. The laws of nature became laws of reason. They were the same always and everywhere. Like the axioms of mathematics, they had only to be made known to be accepted.[2] The meaning of life was rooted in reason, and

1. Archibald MacLeish, *J.B.* (New York: Samuel French, 1956), p. 18.
2. Basil Willey, *The Eighteenth Century Background* (Boston: Beacon Press, 1961), p. 2.

reason was not only imposed on all of life, it was also read into it. The world was inherently a rational universe, an orderly cosmos which could be understood by reason.

With the success of the physical sciences, based as they were on a wedding of nature and mathematics, modern man began to apply the devices of reason to every other field of human experience. Even the absurdities and irrationalities of history were made amenable to the strictures of logic. Some historians saw historical events as "logical transactions set out on a time-scale."[3] The German historians made Germany the center of the logical process. The communists saw themselves as the conclusion of a rational development. The British saw logic in the course of empire, and the Americans tried to impose on the ambiguities of history the rationality of their own manifest destiny.

Modern civilization is the result of the attempt to impose reason not only on the brute realities of nature but also on the raw experience of man. For men reared in the first half of the twentieth century this is at heart a reasonable universe. If it does not now seem reasonable, it will eventually be shown to be so. The faith of modern man has been that eventually all the present absurdities and mysteries will be explained within the syllogisms of logic. Wars, epidemics, political catastrophes, diseases, and even the weather will finally be explained.

The particular type of reason that has held sway is modeled after the myth of the machine. The ancient Hebrews believed in their naiveté that the world was really a giant tent; modern man in his enlightenment has believed it to be a giant machine. The Hebrews believed that their world of the tent was the habitation of man; with the world-machine, man became merely a spectator

3. R. G. Collingwood, *The Idea of History* (New York: Oxford University Press, 1956), p. 117.

rather than a participant in the universe. Man did not fit the machine, and when he could not be made to fit the Procrustean bed of a mechanistic logic, he was cut down as irrational.

The plight of a man trying to write a letter to a computer about his bill, the displacement of names with numbers, the electronic escalation of a war—all are prime examples of the ruthless imposition of a mechanistic reason upon the vagaries of human experience. If a man cannot make the computer understand, he is liable to lose his credit card and even his credit rating. If he cannot remember his identification number but still knows his name, he may be condemned to wander the face of the earth without a home.

One of the ironies of the modern era is that the more the rationalistic system of modern civilization has dismissed man as irrational, the more he has placed his hope in it. And the more he has placed his hope in it, the more that hope has been frustrated by the absurdity of events. The terrors and tumults of the twentieth century are the result of human absurdity, not of the illogic of nature. No computer, however complex and sophisticated, can do justice to the wonderful vagaries and awful absurdities of human experience.

Rationalism has produced a humorless type of piety called idealism. Idealism is the attempt to impose a moral logic and meaning on human experience. It often afflicts the young, but surprisingly many older people attempt to palm it off also. The moral ideal of racial justice is made an absolute good, for instance, and the idealist spends his life and sees his meaning in the imposition of that ideal upon the political, social, and economic ambiguities of his era. The belief is that if men and women know better, they will be better. Therefore, if the ethical ideal is presented to them, they will respond with changed behavior. The difficulty is that the good is not always so apparent as the idealists would have us believe, nor is it always so easy of realization. Idealism usually collapses when it is forced to confront the brute realities of social absurdity.

The result is often a cynic, for a cynic is really an idealist gone sour. He still holds to his ideals. The problem is that in his mind everyone else, or nearly everyone else, is a fraud. Having found the world unyieldingly resistant to his ethical logic, he rejects the world and holds to the illusion that he alone, and perhaps a few of his favored colleagues, exemplify moral goodness. The cynic has the perverse habit of always escaping the imprecations he hurls at society.

Just as there is little laughter in mathematics, so there is little humor found among the idealists and cynics, for humor is built upon the foundation of incongruity, the rock of absurdity. Just as a geometric axiom is not likely to produce gales of laughter, so the ethical rationalist is not likely to see much humor in the surds that confound him. Absurdity for the idealist is an occasion for bafflement; for the man of faith it is an occasion for either faith or laughter.

Like humor, faith presupposes two fundamental human experiences—grace and incongruity. Faith arises from the profound incongruities of life, the tragedies, and humor from the everyday absurdities. If a man responds to tragedy with a sense of grace, that response is one of faith. He believes that tragedy is not ultimate. If he responds without grace, however, then tragedy becomes a tutor of despair. If all a man has is a sense of tragedy, then he has no place to go. A sense of the ultimate graciousness of life is the quality that renders tragedy a tutor of faith.

Humor rests on a sense of grace as well as of the absurd. Many things pass for humor in our society which in fact are better classed under the category of ridicule and rejection. Poking fun at someone has its roots in bitterness, not grace. A racial joke told by a person of a different race is a form of ridicule and hostility, but the very same joke told by someone of the same race is of a different quality. A Jewish joke told by a Jewish comedian assumes a sense of grace and love for the Jews, and it also points out their absurdities. It is told with both judgment and fondness. The same joke told by a Nazi is a different story altogether, and it is not nearly so funny. Bitterness as a quality of laughter does not take long to turn sour, and that which was supposed to sweeten life leaves only an acid taste in the mouth.

Humor, if it is creative and redemptive, assumes a quality of grace. The reason that genuine humor has fallen on such hard times is not only the rationalistic malaise of modern civilization but also its loss of grace. About the only laughter found today among the intellectuals, the chief keepers of idealism, is a bitter irony, a ridicule of their opponents. It does not redeem, re-create, or even cleanse. It abuses.

A sense of humor, then, is a little faith. The difficulty with many Christians of a rationalistic frame of mind is that they always look at life under the category of the ultimate. They have no place for the minor incongruities that form the substance of life. How does one respond to a husband who always seems to make somewhat of an idiot of himself at parties? What is the appropriate response to a wife whose sense of high fashion never seems to befit her circumstances? How does one cope with all of the eccentricities of adolescence?

The little faith of humor is as much a part of authentic piety as the great faith of tragedy, for a sense of humor gives one the capacity to get through life graciously, creatively, and redemptively. It allows the believer to react with grace to the incongruous, especially when the incongruous is himself. If a doctor cannot laugh at the American Medical Association, he is in bad shape. If a minister cannot chuckle at the pious pretenses of the church, he is in for some bad years. If a union steward cannot see the humor in labor's claims, he is liable to be a bore. Like faith, humor is vital to life.

The difficulty with idealism is that it is done in by absurdity. Rather than using it, idealism must master it, for absurdity is a denial of its existence. The agony of this attitude is that it in no way corresponds to human experience. The idealist makes a fatal assumption about man: he assumes that man is perfectible. He actually believes that a man can live up to his ideals, that he can fulfill existentially his rational expectations.

Idealism has become so rampant in modern society that many would tie it to the church. And many in the church would have it this way. The phrase "a fine Christian young man" generally means a young man filled with moral ideals. Indeed, one suspects that much of the mission work of the church has been done by young people so corrupted. But any style of piety that does not equip a man gracefully to cope with the nonsense of life is a mistake. More than that, it is a profound corruption if it teaches that the thin tissue of logic can cover the grievous wounds of mankind.

There is a grave fatality to idealism, for it would have it that man can be improved without first being loved, that his absurdities are intolerable, that he is indeed an object for moral manipulation. When man does not yield to the pressure of a manipulative moralism, then he is rejected. There is about as much place for man in the world of the ethical idealist as there was in the world-machine of Sir Isaac Newton.

Idealism is essentially a pagan endeavor, for although it is sometimes dressed up in Christian vocabulary, it is still at bottom an attempt to save man by his own wisdom and purity. Since it is founded on reason rather than faith, and beholds absurdity as the final assault on man's meaning, those who accept it cannot have a sense of humor. They live with the gracelessness of those whose very lives hang on themselves.

The disillusioned idealist often becomes the fanatical "true believer" who attempts to impose meaning on life with a holy cause. When the neat syllogisms of the rationalist disintegrate under the pressure of events, he tends to become either a quiet, intellectual cynic or an activist, a "true believer." The one gives up, while the other continues to impose meaning, not by rationality, but by commitment to one ultimate and unsullied cause. The difficulty is that finally "hatred becomes a habit."[4]

Again, some would have even this become the purpose of the church. Many so-called committed Christians have the same air of moral rectitude as the fanatic. The capacity to forgive, much less laugh, is lost, for the purpose is no longer to redeem but to straighten out. To tolerate ambiguity and incongruity a sense of grace is required. The true believer, like the idealist, lacks this sense, and so he ends up hating them, for they stand in the way of his imposing meaning on life by the fiat of his holy cause. The idealist tries to impose meaning by the goodness of his life, the true believer by the finality of his truth.

A sense of the grace of life is the awareness that one's meaning and substance are a gift, not an accomplishment. The gift is a loving relationship in which one lives solely by the love of the other. A child's security requires the freely given love of his parents. A husband's sense of well-being depends upon the constancy of his wife's affection. The heart of grace is a relation-

4. Eric Hoffer, *The True Believer* (New York: Harper and Row, 1951), p. 145.

ship, a relationship of love. As such, it is always a gift, for one never earns someone's love. It is always given, for if it is earned, it is killed. A gracious wife is one well loved by a husband. A gracious child is one deeply loved by parents. The debonaire disciple is one who lives by the love of God in Jesus Christ. Unlike the idealist, the cynic, and the true believer, he has a sense of grace, and he has a sense of humor.

Man's search for meaning, which is a quest for a style of life pertinent to the times, must finally come to terms with life's ambiguity. Speaking out of the horrors of Nazi concentration camps, Viktor Frankl has observed: "What is demanded of man is not, as some existential philosophers teach, to endure the meaninglessness of life; but rather to bear his incapacity to grasp its unconditional meaningfulness in rational terms. *Logos* is deeper than logic."[5] The motifs characteristic of the twentieth century do not yield themselves to the syllogisms of rationality. Rather, the dominant note is one of absurdity and incongruity. Indeed, one might say that the attempt to reason one's way into meaning is always doomed to failure because life is always contingent upon man's biases and affections, and they are irrational.

Perhaps the man most responsible for pointing out the fundamental absurdity of life in our modern era has been the French author Albert Camus. He wrote: "Today the great passions of unity and liberty disrupt the world. Yesterday love led to individual death. Today collective passions make us run the risk of universal destruction."[6] The absurdity of which Camus spoke was that of society, rather than of nature, in relationship to man. In other words, it was a historical absurdity. "The absurdity which is pictured to us is not that of man before a

5. Viktor E. Frankl, *Man's Search for Meaning* (New York: Washington Square Press, 1963), pp. 187 f.
6. Albert Camus, *Resistance, Rebellion and Death,* trans. Justin O'Brien (New York: Alfred A. Knopf, 1961), pp. 237 f.

senseless and fragmentary nature which is foreign to
him as a human being; rather, the absurdity is in the
attempt of society justly to apply absolute moral stan-
dards to the uncertain and chartless course of human
life."[7]

A classic example of this can be found in the story of
Job, in which a man suffers for no apparent reason and
is made to suffer further by the attempt of his three
friends to impose upon his chaos a rule of moral reason.
Their rationalism does not assuage his grief but exacerbates it, just as rationalism exacerbates the suffering
of modern man. Idealism as a piety is the luxury of the
untouched; it cannot be afforded by those who have
been touched by the terrors and tumults of modern
civilization.

Moral idealism and its progenitor, rationalism, suffer
from another shortcoming, that of being unable to illuminate human experience. A good sense of humor not only
springs from a sense of absurdity and an experience of
grace, it also throws the light of understanding upon the
foibles of human experience. A shock of recognition
takes place when one realizes that the joke is, in the
end, on the one who laughs. Idealism tries to cram
human experience into a preconceived set of rules that
are irrelevant to it. A sense of humor begins where the
experience is. It takes man as he is and starts from
there. Humor thus can illuminate a man's life, for it
enables him to see under the aegis of grace what his life
is really like.

The pretenses, pomposities, ruses, and frauds that
make up so much of human experience are exposed by
humor, and in such a way that one laughs at them in
oneself rather than in others. Listening to a Jewish joke
told by a Jewish storyteller, for instance, one has the

7. Thomas Hanna, *The Thought and Art of Albert Camus* (Chicago:
Henry Regnery Co., 1958), p. 55.

endearing and infectious experience of seeing someone laugh at himself in a loving way. It is not a form of self-denigration but of affection and redemption. Also, while still laughing one begins to realize that the eccentricity revealed in the story is not confined to the Jews but is indeed a universal human characteristic. The Jewish story then becomes a universal story in which every man can find his place. The humor becomes redemptive and creative. It does not abuse. Rather, it offers the possibility of renewal.

The experience of seeing one's own faults, or those of mankind in general, is often called humility. It involves the recognition that most of man's problems and dilemmas are unavoidable. The character flaws and eccentricities picked up by most people in childhood and adolescence can seldom be eradicated. Children with any spunk will never be so docile as to devote themselves to pleasing their mother. One's wife will never be as efficient as one's secretary.

The problem is that most people approach life having been thoroughly corrupted by idealism. If they manage to escape the pitfalls of cynicism and fanaticism, it is because they have a sense of absurdity and grace, not only about others but also about themselves. This gives them the capacity not only to endure the ironies in their lives but also to prevail over them by enjoying them. They can enjoy them because their lives are illuminated and given new understanding by humor.

Any authentic Christian piety must finally come to terms with the cross, an event which was an absurdity, for in it the goodness and justice of man—Jewish piety and Roman law—put to death the graciousness of God. Absurdity is no stranger to the Christian faith, for the cross is the absurdity where the Christian begins. He certainly does not start with the rationality of his own goodness. Rather, he begins with his own ambiguity and the absurdity of the cross, which Paul calls the "foolishness of God."

One thing which distinguishes both faith and humor is a sense of the holy. A person can laugh at the everyday problems of life, but before the final problems laughter is inappropriate and destructive. Before the cross of Christ, a joke is impertinent. Indeed, people who laugh in the presence of the holy have displayed their incapacity to laugh in the presence of the everyday. They cannot cope with absurdity because they have no sense of grace. They attempt to dismiss with laughter something that must grasp them with finality.

To be a man of little faith, one must first of all be a man of profound faith. The capacity to respond with humor to all the petty ironies of life takes a faith that has first faced life's tragic dimension and has lived through it with the experience of grace. The cross of Christ has a double message. It points both to the tragic absurdity of mankind and to the graciousness of God in the face of that tragedy. Absurdity is not the final word, for out of tragedy comes the message of mercy.

Paul said: "Where is the wise man? Where is the scribe? Where is the debater of this age? Has not God made foolish the wisdom of the world? For since, in the wisdom of God, the world did not know God through wisdom, it pleased God through the folly of what we preach to save those who believe. For Jews demand signs and Greeks seek wisdom, but we preach Christ crucified, a stumbling block to Jews and folly to Gentiles, but to those who are called, both Jews and Greeks, Christ the power of God and the wisdom of God. For the foolishness of God is wiser than men, and the weakness of God is stronger than men" (1 Cor. 1:20–25).

In the folly and weakness of the cross God revealed his grace, so that man can respond to absurdity within the milieu of mercy. Just as faith is man's response in grace to the ultimate tragedies, so humor is man's response in grace to the everyday incongruities. "The intimate relation between humor and faith is derived from the fact that both deal with the incongruities of our existence. Humor is concerned with the immediate incongruities of life, and faith with ultimate ones."[8]

Humor is in fact a prelude to faith and is fulfilled in faith. It is an illuminated and creative mixture of judgment and mercy. It enables one to bear incongruity without being destroyed by it. When parents laugh at the adolescent pretenses of their children, they are not rejecting them but forbearing with them with love. Their laughter is an expression of grace.

Laughter and tears in a human being are very close. Much of life is a wavering between the two, between faith and despair. The force that tips the balance is the presence of grace. Life is ambiguous. It is an amalgam of good and evil, triumph and tragedy. But one must decide which elements of the ambiguity are ultimate. The debonaire disciple is one who has chosen the gracious relationships of mercy as the source of his meaning. His faith is rooted in the folly and scandal of the cross, and he lives this faith in God's mercy in a world of absurdities and incongruities.

Rather than sobriety being a hallmark of a graceful style of life, it may be that laughter and humor are much more often to the point. The idealist consumes a great deal of his energy in indignation and self-righteousness, vices which are not rewarding. The cynic snaps and snarls through life pumping more acid into his system than it was designed to take and learning nothing about himself in the process. The graceful man can laugh because his humor is a prelude to his faith, a faith born of an awareness of absurdity and an experience of grace.

8. Reinhold Niebuhr, *Discerning the Signs of the Times* (London: SCM Press, 1946), pp. 99 f.

CHAPTER 5

SLIPPING THE FETTERS

"It was one of those southern nights under whose spell all the sterner energies of the mind cloak themselves and lie down in bivouac, and the fancy and imagination, that cannot sleep, slip their fetters and escape, beckoned away from behind every flowering bush and sweet-smelling tree, and every stretch of lonely, half-lighted walk, by the genius of poetry."[1] Such a flight of imagination would be dismissed by a rationalistic, computerized culture as mere sentiment. It would be put down as maudlin emotionalism, for just as the computer has no place for wonder, so the child of reason has no place for mystery and awe.

A sense of absurdity is in some ways the obverse of a sense of mystery. The latter is the awareness that life is greater than the syllogism. It is the sense of wonder and awe that overcomes a man when he finds that the tidy structures of his mind cannot in the end comprehend the grandeur of life. The rationalist cashiers mystery from the ranks of the intellectually respectable on the grounds of weak-mindedness. The debonaire disciple sees it as the beginning of wisdom.

The neat, rationalistic mind which has been dominant in modern civilization has been characterized by the dogma that all truth is knowable within its own frame of

1. George W. Cable, "Madame Delphine," in *The Scribner Treasury* (New York: Charles Scribner's Sons, 1953), p. 30.

reference. The truth has thus been made into an intellectual formula, and so mystery, awe, and absurdity have become threats rather than delights. The church has often reflected this rigid habit of mind by attempting to place all the mysteries of God and the absurdities of man in neat little creedal rows. The Christian came to be distinguished by his right ideas. His mind was fettered by the chains of right doctrine. Seeking security in the castle of correct beliefs, he raised the drawbridge to mystery and found himself isolated from wonder, awe, and finally worship.

The traditional piety has thus often been characterized by a need for truth as well as a desire for goodness. The Christian was the man who strove for the right answers and the pure life. The aim was improvement, but the fallacy of improvement is that once a person has improved, he becomes better than someone who hasn't improved. The ground is dangerous when a man thinks he is better and knows better than others. Rather than seeing his ideas as possible points of view, he looks upon them as final and fixed truths.

The Christian is not the only one who has been victimized by this rationalistic desire for rigidity. The whole of the computerized culture has also suffered from it. The emotional and intellectual aridity of modern society is effective witness to the dogmatism that has infected nearly every part of society. Eyes do not dance with expectancy when everything is laid out on a syllogistic grid. In response to this rationalistic oppressiveness there have been various attempts at protest among the young, the disenchanted, and the dispossessed, but they have been futile or merely palliative. They may have satisfied the need to protest, but they have not changed the essentially rationalistic quality of modern culture. An emotionally satisfying but ineffective protest in the long run makes a mockery of its point and turns the idealistic protesters into cynics.

Most societies are organized on an anti- or non-Christian basis. They try to manipulate or coerce the citizens by means of some sort of cultural approval which the people will work to earn. This is generally accomplished by getting the people to accept some rationalistic system of meaning that forms the heart of the culture. In such a system, the debonaire disciple is always a sheep amidst the wolves, for the meaning of his life comes from a different source than does the culture's. His meaning is given freely by Jesus Christ. It is not the reward of unquestioning service on the culture's treadmill.

Mystery and absurdity are thus not only challenges to the rationalistic system of meaning of a given culture; they are also threats to the organization of society. If a man marches to a different drummer, there is not much a social organization can do to lure, reward, or coerce him. He is free.

The sense of absurdity which is part of the life of faith and humor is a threat and a frustration to a rationalistic mind, because it denies that there is a rational explanation of everything. Mystery, however, is an even greater threat to rationalism, for it implies that the final meaning of life is a riddle which is inexplicable by syllogisms. In contrast to this, mystery is at the heart of the Christian experience, in which it is seen as a fundamental affirmation of life. For the rationalist the resurrection of Jesus Christ is an absurdity because it does not fit his program of syllogisms, but from the place of faith it is a mystery which affirms life in the context of its apparent denial in the crucifixion.

Much of traditional piety, Roman Catholic as well as Protestant, made the mistake of trying to replace this sense of mystery with a list of true doctrines and beliefs. Behind this attempt in the Protestant piety has been the presupposition that God reveals himself in doctrines and dogmas. This is a severe intellectualization of faith. Indeed, it is almost a salvation by knowledge, according to which God has revealed himself in absolute truths enshrined in the Scriptures and all one has to do to be saved is to know these truths. As Dietrich Bonhoeffer has pointed out, doctrine became a substitute for the reality to which the doctrine was supposedly pointing, namely, God himself. "Cheap grace means grace as a doctrine, a principle, a system. It means forgiveness of sins proclaimed as a general truth, the love of God taught as the Christian 'conception' of God. An intellectual assent to that idea is held to be of itself sufficient to secure remission of sins. The church which holds the correct doctrine of grace, has it is supposed, *ipso facto* a part in the grace."[2]

If God's revelation is information about himself, then the Bible becomes a book containing all of these accurate and true statements about God. Now, oddly enough, even the liberals who reacted against the literalism of much of the traditional piety accepted the fundamentalist doctrine of revelation. Their objection was not that revelation was seen as a series of true doctrines about God but that much of the Bible was primitive and needed updating because of human enlightenment.

Any attempt at a renewal of piety which will be in accord with both the gospel and the times must come to terms with the way God makes himself known to man. One has to reexamine the beliefs undergirding that piety, especially the doctrine of revelation. It would

2. Dietrich Bonhoeffer, *The Cost of Discipleship*, trans. R. H. Fuller (New York: Macmillan Co., 1959), p. 35.

seem obvious that the way one phrases and understands his ideas is conditioned by his time. Some ideas and doctrines have a continuing validity, but the way they were originally expressed affects the way they are understood. One central assumption of the Christian experience is the grace of God, his constantly giving and loving relationship with man no matter what manner of madness man might be engaged in. A doctrine of grace is the attempt intellectually to understand this experience, but it is not grace itself. Grace itself is the gracious presence of God in Christ.

Doctrine is essentially an afterthought, a process of thinking that takes place after the experience, in which a man tries to understand what happened to him. Always the experience is larger than the capacities of the mind, and therefore understanding is always partial and fragmented. Life is larger than syllogisms, and while syllogisms may be necessary to understand experience, they are a pitiful substitute for the real thing. The grace of God is not really an "it," but a "he," and theology is merely the human attempt to grasp the meaning of that person in our lives.

The effectiveness of a doctrine lies in its ability to enlighten our experience, to enlarge our understanding of what has happened to us, to help us grasp the essence of what we have lived through. A doctrine is really a signpost pointing to something or someone else. A young woman in her first years of marriage is likely to recall, many times unconsciously, something of her parents' marriage. If the ideas of marriage and family life which she has developed during her childhood help her understand the dynamics of her own marriage, then her ideas are acting as signposts. However, if she lets those ideas dominate her marriage, then she will force herself into her mother's mold and will try to coerce her husband into her father's mold. She will, of course, have no marriage. She will have used ideas as a substitute for relationship.

The value of theology, then, is not in telling us what to believe, but in helping us understand through the experience of others what has happened to us. Great people with great minds often explain things in such a fashion that our experiences and our conceptions of them take on new and deeper meanings. If a man is to grow, he must listen to others talk of their experience of Jesus Christ.

Since revelation is God's response to man's plight, it will be influenced by the kind of questions man asks. If we accept an antivice ethics, then we have assumed that morally man's problem is his own personal purity. If we think that revelation is a series of doctrines, then we have assumed that man's problem is fundamentally his ignorance. Neither of these assumptions is biblically faithful, however, for man's fundamental problem is his alienation from God. The story in the second and third chapters of Genesis is that of man's attempt to live without God. Truth, beauty, and goodness were enough for him.

If man's plight is his attempt to live as if God were not, that is, by his own values and ideals, then he does not need more ideas about God, he needs God himself. The stuff of revelation is not ideas about God, but God himself. This is why the Christian's understanding of Jesus Christ as God in flesh is so important, for in Jesus the Christian seeks and finds the presence of God himself in his revelation, rather than settling for some secondhand surrogate.

Theology, then, is not a set of everlastingly true doctrines but the attempt of the church in each age to understand the meaning of God's presence. The Bible is the word of God, but not because it contains a series of inerrantly true ideas about God, Christ, man, and the world. It is an interpretive record of what God has done to reveal himself. Since Jesus Christ was the culmination of that revelation, the authority or power of the Bible does not rest in itself but in its power to witness to the real revelation of God, namely, Jesus Christ.

The analogy of a record player might be useful here. The disc is a record of a live performance. Like all records it may have some distortions, but a listener can hear the music without getting distracted by them. The original musical message was in the mind of the composer. He transcribed that message on paper, and the performance of the transcribed music was recorded on a disc. The result of this process is a record which is really a signpost pointing to the mind and heart of the composer. It is a witness to his genius and vision. Of course, the ability of the listener to appreciate the original musical message depends partly on the limitations of his phonograph and his own hearing capacities.

The word of God is like the genius of the composer. When its message gets across to the listener, his life is ennobled and renewed, and that is the value of the "music." The Bible is like the record. Some distortions occur in the performance of the "music" and in the making of the record. Others occur when the record is played and heard. However, anyone who loves the music and its message can generally sort these out. The tunes of glory of the Bible are so simple and so pertinent to man that even a poor phonograph and a bad ear cannot keep one from tapping his toe.

In addition to being unfaithful to the Bible, the idea that God reveals himself in ideas does not really fit man's experience. For brief times men may think that their problem is ignorance, but certainly the cry of contemporary man, especially the young, is for authenticity in relationships, not their intellectualization. Like a computer, modern man is adept at storing information, but he hasn't shown much ability at becoming a human being.

If the relationship between God and man is essentially personal, then the communication between God and man must be historical, for history is the realm of persons. The I-thou encounter of God with man means that God reveals himself, not ideas about himself. The ideas are the product of human reflection upon that encounter, and it is a serious mistake to reverse the process and say that the revelation is the ideas and not the person.

One of the meanings of the ascension of our Lord is that he is no longer confined to a particular cultural milieu but can relate to all men everywhere in their peculiar situations. Thus the authority of the Scriptures does not reside in their literal statements, which reflect a particular Jewish culture. Rather, their authority rests in their witness to God's self-disclosure in Jesus Christ. This means that the Bible is not a textbook of faith, but rather a record of God's decisive revelation of himself in a particular setting. Even in the Bible theological statements are historically relative. Their authority rests in their relationship to the word of God in Jesus Christ.

A good bit of the traditional piety has missed this point and fallen into the error of thinking that God ultimately reveals himself in statements which are absolutely true. If God, on the other hand, reveals himself in events of history, then theological statements are neither true nor false. They are merely adequate or inadequate in explaining the meaning of the divine-human encounters in any given age. In other words, theology is liberated from the burden of absolute truth and can attempt instead to be adequate for a given time.

An interpretation of the meaning of the gospel must have both authenticity and pertinence to be adequate. The difficulty with making claims of final truth is that it often means that believers are required to assent to theological propositions which may have been faithful to the gospel in a former day but which make little if any sense in the present. One of the crushing burdens of the modern church is its boredom, which is partly due to the irrelevance of much of the old theological apparatus. To the modern ear this is often mumbo jumbo, yet there are those who will defend it to the death because of its "absolute truth."

The heart and core of the Christian life is not a series of everlastingly true doctrines. It is the presence of Jesus Christ himself, to which the doctrines are attempting to bear witness by means of understanding. This understanding is tested not by its truth but by its adequacy in pointing to the reality of Jesus Christ today. The incarnation is God's relativity to man, and the truth of the Christian faith is not in theological abstractions but in the relativity of God to man. If Jesus Christ is the truth, he is the truth of faithful graciousness, not intellectual abstraction.

Both theology and piety have suffered because of the intellectualization of the church's theology. In theology it has led to the assumption of fixed claims of truth, which destroys dialogue and growth. In piety it has led to the belief that faith is mental assent to doctrines — which puts a straitjacket on the mind. The proper purpose of theology in relationship to piety is the clarification and explanation of the meaning of the relationship between God and man. As such it is an afterthought. It is thinking after the experience to give meaning to the experience. This means that theology is the function of every Christian and not merely the special domain of a few so-called theologians.

Because of the truth claims of much of theology, we have been led to believe that skepticism and agnosticism are wrong. If one adopts the position outlined above, however, one will see that these attitudes are hallmarks of an authentic piety, not threats to it. Skepticism is the position which recognizes that there is a difference between appearance and reality, between what is claimed and what is. In an age of advertising and propaganda, it is a virtue which is necessary for survival. Its opposite is credulity, which is almost always a vice — perhaps one of Augustine's "splendid vices."

Skepticism may resemble cynicism, but in reality they are very different. Cynicism is the product of disillusionment. Skepticism, on the other hand, is the product of a discovery, a discovery at once of the graciousness of God and the malaise of man. It is the awareness of the need for caution when someone else claims to have the truth, and of the need for repentance when one thinks one has it oneself.

Our Lord instructed his disciples to be as innocent as doves and as wise as serpents, because they were going out as sheep among the wolves. The faithful skepticism of the debonaire disciple is that serpentine savvy which our Lord encouraged us to develop. The integrity of the believer hangs on God's relationship to him, not on his ability to believe the best of his society. The carefree quality of the Christian life is the result of God's graciousness in Jesus Christ, not of a trust in wolves.

Agnosticism is simply the knowledge that one does not finally know. It has always been the attitude of any adequate Protestant theology. Thus when Calvin said that one does not know God in himself but only as he relates to us, he was adopting an agnostic position. Unfortunately, Protestant theology — especially that associated with the traditional piety — has often abandoned this position, instead making claims for the absolute truth of its doctrines.

Part of the boredom of the traditional piety is the result of its lack of a sense of mystery and wonder. This lack is often blamed on the scientific age, but it could just as well be blamed on the claims of truth made by the theology of this piety. A completed syllogism is not mysterious, and there is no wonder in a neatly wrapped system. Mystery and wonder go hand in hand with agnosticism, with the knowledge that claims of truth evaporate in the face of God's sovereignty. The man who realizes that nothing can ever be finally said about God lives with a sense of mystery and wonder. He accepts the fact that he cannot fully understand the graciousness of God, that he does not fully know. He simply rejoices.

The church has often described God in himself with such words as "infinite," "eternal," and "unchangeable." Alfred North Whitehead calls these "metaphysical compliments." They say nothing at all about God. They only refer to our ignorance, that is to say, they point out that God is beyond the limits of our comprehension—which is what agnosticism claims. A man lives by faith and not by knowledge, a fact which Paul pointed out some time ago but which many Christians have forgotten in their desire for the security of absolute knowledge. The desire for final truths is the desire to live without faith. If faith is central to an authentic piety, then a faithful agnosticism cannot help but be an integral part of such a piety.

Credulity in accepting the authoritative teachings of the church was often an element of the traditional piety. In the name of piety nonsense was foisted off on believers; they were required to believe abstract truths which often meant little to them. Doubt and agnosticism in relationship to these absolute truths were considered evil, and thus what are indeed virtues to a piety were treated as evils.

Skepticism is related to humility as agnosticism is related to wonder. The Christian cannot claim to have absolute truth; he must always treat his own theological formulations as well as the claims and assertions of others with the hesitancy of skepticism. In an age of propaganda and advertising, skepticism is not a luxury but a necessity. Without it a person will be inundated and tyrannized by society. His integrity will be devastated.

The integrity of the believer is born of God's graciousness, and thus it is not something for which he struggles and which he achieves. It is the gift of God, and only in the assurance of this graciousness can one have the courage of agnosticism and skepticism. Credulity and acceptance of authoritative teaching are marks of those who are searching for the security of a ready-made integrity and meaning. The security of the true believer is also the security of destruction of the person. It is the security of tyranny. Such a tyrannical security cannot allow skepticism and agnosticism.

The Christian lives in a milieu of graciousness, and in this milieu he can have the courage of agnosticism and skepticism. He begins with a wonder at the graciousness of God, which he cannot explain but which he experiences. Because of this his life is marked by faith and humor, by a believing skepticism and agnosticism, and by rejoicing. He doesn't have to be right. He already is, not by his truth, but by the truth of God's graciousness.

CHAPTER 6

INNOCENTS ABROAD

Since the debonaire disciple begins at the place most men strive to reach, his attitude toward life is different from theirs. He does not have to earn anything, because he already has all he needs. His life is a gift. His mind is freed from the burden of constantly trying to prove how much he knows. Intellectually he is free to explore, to seek out, to test and try the parade of surprises that passes through every man's life. Emotionally he is freed from the straitjacket of correct feelings. He can afford to laugh and cry and not be ashamed. The strengh of his life does not consist in the nonemotive facade favored by so-called mature people, but rather in a God-given confidence.

The debonaire disciple is also free ethically. He is no longer forced to prove how good he is. He is free to use effective ethics, rather than defensive ethics. Traditionally the personal morality of the middle class has been defensive and antivice. It has been aimed at keeping oneself pure by fighting off the vices that afflict everyone. Morality thus became a largely negative affair in which one strove to avoid corruptions in order to prove one's acceptability. The traditional piety adopted this outlook, adding a quest for absolute goodness to its striving for absolute truth.

The malaise of this kind of ethics is twofold. First, it turns a person inward. His purpose in life becomes the maintenance of his own purity. Second, it is impossible and irrelevant. Most of the situations in which people find themselves are so laden with ambiguity that the desire to be pure pretty much removes a man from life. If a person actually thinks that he has become pure, he is deluding himself. The essential ambiguity of life prevents purity.

A person who adopted this moral outlook was often forced into a physical or emotional monasticism in which his aim was to escape from the world. The believer was supposed to live as if the world did not exist, all the while condemning the secularist for living as if God did not exist. One is about as bad and addled as the other. The believer ceased to be pertinent to the world for which Christ died.

Ironically, one of the biblical texts used by the traditional pietists actually contradicted their aims: "You, therefore, must be perfect, as your heavenly Father is perfect" (Matt. 5:48). For the pietists perfection meant being without moral blemish. It was fundamentally a negative idea. But the Greek word which is translated as "perfect" means accomplished, complete, or fulfilled in the New Testament. The aim advocated in the biblical passage is integrity and authenticity, not purity.

The traditional moral perfectionism led inevitably to the addition of "counsels" and "precepts" to the gospel. The aim was to instruct people into perfection. Another irony of this view is that once a person has deluded himself that he has reached this supposedly blessed state, he really no longer needs the gospel. In effect, much of the traditional piety replaced the good news of God's graciousness with the bad news of moral perfection.

The moral outlook of the traditional piety also implied that the Christian life was basically a series of external acts. A believer was designated by what he did rather than by who he was. Ethics became a code of behavior, the chief aim of which was to give one rules by which one could prove oneself worthy. As such it was a denial of the heart of the Christian faith, which is a relationship between God and man based solely on God's graciousness and not on a series of rules to be obeyed.

Our Lord sends the debonaire disciple out into the world with the injunction mentioned before, that he must be as innocent as a dove and as wise as a serpent. This dovelike innocence is a gift from God. It is the perfection of integrity and wholeness that comes from a lively and vital relationship with God. The old-style perfectionist assumed that dovelike innocence was the product of his own moral rectitude, an integrity achieved through goodness. As such, it was also sound middle-class American morality. Whether the American culture dominated the church or the church the American culture at this point is not clear. Perhaps it was a bit of both, but the result has been the same. Rather than the carefree quality essential to a genuinely good life, modern man has been supplied with the ethical surrogate of moral success, the "perfection" of the man on the moral make. The final result of such an achievement-oriented outlook is the desperation of the man who is always trying to prove himself, whether through the acquisition of money or the piling up of goodness.

Within the biblical framework the innocence of the dove means the gift of integrity. A man will ultimately feel himself worthwhile—which is the heart of integrity—only on the basis of affirmative and loving human relationships. A man can accept himself because someone else has accepted him. For most human beings this feeling of acceptance begins with parental love, but ultimately it must come from the God and Father of all men. Human love is an ephemeral thing unless it is set within the ultimate context of God's love.

A sense of integrity is the beginning of ethics, not the result. If it is the result, then ethics is really no more than a carefully calculated selfishness in which one does things to get things. If it is the beginning of ethics, then ethics is no longer a series of rules by which one gains respectability, but rather a set of guides by which one expresses his integrity. Christian ethics thus presupposes what non-Christian ethics desires to achieve.[1]

The ethics of the debonaire disciple is less a matter of rules or codes of conduct than of guides in gratitude. When a child misbehaves, the response of the father can be either to lay down the law in an attempt to crush and coerce the child into goodness, or to have a talk on the edge of the bed at night about what counts in life and how much his father and mother love him. Misbehavior is best met with reassurance, not censure. Laying down the law may have the modest advantage of giving vent to the father's frustrations, but as far as the child is concerned, it will render him either spiritlessly docile or defiantly hostile. It will not set him straight.

If ethics is a guide to gratitude and relationships, then it is more a matter of attitude than of obligatory obedience. In the Sermon on the Mount our Lord constantly makes a matter of internal attitude rules that had previously been external. This internalization of the law was one of the major themes of Jeremiah and the other prophets. Ethics is essentially an attitude rooted in the graciousness of God and in man's response to that graciousness.

The Beatitudes are the best illustration of this graciousness expressed in ethics. Each one begins with a statement of the quality of life of the believer: "Blessed are you." The believer already has the gift of graciousness, and, even in the face of persecution, his response

1. Helmut Thielicke, *Theological Ethics,* trans. William H. Lazareth (Philadelphia: Fortress Press, 1966-), 1:51.

is qualified by that graciousness. The internalization of the law in the Sermon on the Mount is rooted in the *fait accompli* of God's grace in Jesus Christ.

The *fait accompli* of God's graciousness makes possible the innocence of the dove, and Christian ethics or the law of God is properly a tutor to a life in that graciousness. This is a singularly important point in a time when "law and order" has become such a divisive issue. On the one hand, there are some who protest their freedom in such a negative fashion that they indeed become lawless. On the other hand, there are those who are so afraid of making decisions that they subject themselves to a code of ethics in a misbegotten sense of duty. The innocence of the debonaire disciple has no place for such lawlessness or such legalism. He is secure enough in the *fait accompli* of Jesus Christ to be able to distinguish tutors from monitors.

The contemporary lawlessness has two origins. One is a rejection of the blind legalism of many modern bureaucratic institutions. The other is the insecurity of the lawless themselves, which leads them to interpret any outside suggestion as an invasion.

Legalism as an ethical outlook is not much better than lawlessness. It is obviously contrary to both the freedom and the responsibility of man. An unthinking acquiescence to a morality of duty leaves a man with no responsibility for his decisions and no freedom in making them. He simply does what someone else tells him and disengages himself from the results. Ironically, the ethic of duty often claims to be the most responsible in a time of lawlessness, as witnessed by the cries for "law and order" today, but it is in fact acutely irresponsible. It refuses responsibility for the consequences of actions and finds justification only in an obedience to the rules.

The law of God or Christian ethics is not like a monitor but a tutor. It is essentially a teacher of gra-

ciousness, and it bears upon two things. It is concerned
with the integrity of the believer, that is to say, it is a
tutor with respect to his continuing relationship with
God. It is also a tutor with respect to his relationship
with other men, a tutor of the wisdom of the serpent as
well as of the innocence of the dove.

The difficulty with much of traditional Christian ethics was that it was unrelated to the world. So-called
Christian idealism is a case in point. The possibility of
attaining the goal of idealism is nil if this is understood
as the achievement of perfect obedience to laws. About
the only thing striving for such a goal accomplishes is to
make one feel guilty or unworthy, and since most men
begin with that feeling, any addition to it is really unnec-
essary. Furthermore, since the world is not amenable to
these so-called Christian ideals, it must be repudiated,
with the result that the Christian adopts a two-sphere
life: one sphere of ethics for his personal or Christian
life, and another for his public or social life.

Another possible approach to the issue of the Christian in the world is to adopt the world rather than
repudiating it. The tension between integrity and pertinence is lost in an overwhelming desire for the latter,
with a consequent loss of the center of value. In the
words of John, the Christian decides that the best way
to be in the world is also to be of it. The current demand
for ethical relevance is, of course, a justifiable reaction
to the irrelevance of the old piety. However, the un-
worldliness of the traditional piety is in no sense a
justification for the accommodation of the new piety.

The current "new morality" is really a very old morality, for it is an ethical system based on value or
purpose. The values or ends in view are the basis for the
ethical decision. It is a rejection of the ethical system of
duty, which is based on obedience to a code of conduct.
The difficulty with the ethics of purpose or value is that

it subordinates the law and in some cases excludes it. The result is lawlessness. Like the ethics of duty, the ethics of value assumes that the law is a code and that justification rests in how one acts. In the ethics of value one's actions are justified by their fulfillment of the valued goal, while in the ethics of duty one's actions are justified by their correspondence to those prescribed by the code.

The ethics of value is often a prelude to a radical attack upon men. The revolutionary is a case in point. He becomes so committed to his aim that he is quite willing to subordinate even elemental human rights to its accomplishment. The "true believer" as often as not operates with a contempt for man. An ethics of value without the law is generally an introduction to some form of tyranny.

The contrast between an ethics of duty and an ethics of value ignores a salient factor, which is that legalism and value are really different things. As with many disputes, the issue involves a confusion of concepts and terms. In any adequate thinking about ethics, there are four levels to be considered. The first is that of value, the second that of ethical principle, the third that of moral law, and the fourth that of custom.

When a person thinks about ethics, he is ultimately going to concern himself with some question of value. Ethics is involved only where there is something thought to be of value, whether it is the state, the church, a social class, or even one's own daydreams. The reason that murder is an ethical issue is that human beings are considered important. The reason that stealing is an object of concern is that some people think that the ownership of property is something of value.

The highest level of ethics is the source of this evaluation. One such source is mythology. An example of this can be found in the ethics of nazism, much of which was rooted in the myth of the Aryan race. For the debonaire disciple the source of value is found in Jesus Christ. If God could become man, this placed an ultimate and final estimate upon the worth of man.

From one's understanding of the source of value comes the second level of ethics, the ethical principle. The conquest of the American West was justified by the mythology of manifest destiny. The concept of manifest destiny was the source of value, and the conquest of the West was the ethical principle that in turn justified the moral laws regulating the conduct of the settlers. For the Christian the source of value lies in the doctrines of the creation and the incarnation and is in turn the basis for the ethical principle of the ultimate importance of human dignity. From that principle come the moral laws regarding theft, bearing false witness against one's neighbor, and killing.

Moral law, the third level of ethical discourse, is not the same thing as ethical principle. When the ethics of duty is set in opposition to the ethics of value, what is really happening is a contrast between the third and second levels of discourse. Moral laws have meaning only as expressions of a source of value. Without moral laws a source of value is meaningless. An ethical principle without moral laws tends to be used to justify the whim of fashion.

If a man merely obeys the rules, then he is liable to betray the gospel in his blind obedience to abstractions. If he merely follows the good, then his ignorance is liable to lead to a betrayal of the good. However, if he views his life not as an attempt to achieve the good or obey the rules but as a response to God's graciousness, then he is free from the burden of justification and free to respond to the gospel.

The difficulty with relying on moral laws in themselves is that they are not enough. Which is more important, the moral law against killing or the moral law against theft? If one is forced to decide whether to kill one man to preserve the life of another, what course does one take? The moral laws by themselves offer no solution to such dilemmas; they must be decided in light of the ethical principles and the source of value.

Customs are extensions of moral laws into the daily affairs of men, and they generally reflect the times in which people live. They do not have the enduring quality of moral laws, much less ethical principles, and many times great confusion arises when outworn customs are enforced with a zeal really appropriate only to moral laws and ethical principles. The severity of the old laws concerning horse theft was justifiable in frontier days, but it hardly makes sense in the age of the automobile.

The serpentine wisdom of the debonaire disciple consists in his ability to affirm effectively the meaning of the gospel in a world of ambiguity and absurdity. The man of duty attempts to manufacture his meaning by imposing the abstractions of legalism upon the incongruities of life. The man of value attempts to establish his meaning by imposing another abstraction, which he calls the good, upon life. These are both rationalistic attempts to affix meaning by a permanent affirmation, whether of a set of rules or a final end.

The debonaire disciple realizes that meaning is not found in what one does but in who one is. Because of this, he is free to accept compromise, incomplete results, political incongruities, and moral ambiguities. Indeed, the notion of moral ambiguity arises from a tacit acceptance of the finality of moral laws. Things are ambiguous only if I first accept a rigid set of codes.

Some of the new moralism is really essentially negative, since its roots are in a rejection of the old legalism, and thus its so-called freedom is merely a reaction to an imprisonment in the past. The Christian, on the other hand, does not respond to the inadequacies of the past but to the graciousness of God, and thus he can still listen to the past. He can still listen to the law because it is not his lord but his tutor.

Since no law is universally valid, the Christian is going to be involved in the problem of conflicting moral laws. The legalist must always deny that moral laws might conflict, and he does this by denying or subordinating particular moral laws. The great fear of compromise, of having to decide which moral law has priority, found in both the new moralist and the old legalist is rooted in the dread that one might be found wrong. The Christian is free from this burden of being right or wrong. He only has to ask himself the question of efficaciousness. Under the tutelage of his ethical principles and moral laws, his life is efficacious in affirming its meaning under the aegis of the gospel. If he has been found acceptable by God, then his rightness or wrongness is irrelevant to his life.

The great curse of idealism has been the bane of the ethics of the church. The Christian idealist either deluded himself that he had fulfilled his ideals and became outrageously self-righteous, or suffered under the great weight of his inability to live up to his ideals. The true Christian is one who lives without the visible support of ideals but with the invisible support of the graciousness of God. He is free from the illusions of self-righteousness and the burden of unfulfilled ideals. He is free to act responsibly in response to God's mercy in a world of ambiguity and absurdity. Because his meaning is not derived from the rationality of his ethical ideals, the absurdity of the world poses him no threat.

In an absurd world the idealist can easily turn sour and become a cynic. The debonaire disciple is also free from the curse of cynicism, because while he operates amidst the ambiguities of the world, he also firmly believes, under the aegis of the gospel, that God's graciousness will finally triumph. If God conquered absurdity in the cross through the resurrection, then the Christian can live with partialities with some steadiness of spirit. He has the hope that God's power can bring his will to pass in this most ambiguous of worlds. This frees him from the drive for finality and thus frees him to be effective.

The reptilian wisdom of the debonaire disciple has its source in an awareness of the ambiguity of all moral decisions and a recognition of the pervasive destructiveness of the world. A Christian can never escape the realization that the best of society, Roman law and Jewish religion, put to death the graciousness of God. Being a debonaire disciple does not mean that he is credulous about men. It means that he trusts in God.

The great ethical problem of our time is to keep going with some meaning without getting bogged down in a polite despair or a snarling cynicism. Both of these reactions are derived from an attitude that places too much confidence in man and not enough in God. To the inveterate idealist and the bitter cynic the Christian may appear to be a lunatic. But then lunacy often seems like drunkenness, a charge frequently brought against the early Christians. An innocent abroad may appear to be either a lunatic or a drunk, but he belongs abroad in the world that God loved, a world filled with ambiguities and incongruities. And he belongs there as an innocent, that is, as one who trusts in God's graciousness and is responding to it. He can afford to be in the world without despair and cynicism because his meaning has already been given him. Ethically his life is a gift and not a task.

CHAPTER 7

A DIALOGUE OF DISCOVERY

Isolation in both ancient and modern times has been one of the most refined methods of torture. The assumption behind using it as a punishment is that any man — no matter how strong — who is left alone long enough will finally capitulate. He will either crack up or break down. Being a social animal, he cannot bear sustained isolation. It is an exquisite form of torture, for while it leaves the body intact, the mind is destroyed and the will broken.

The demonic hounds that pursue every man become all the more fearsome on the moors of loneliness. Private terrors and inner hells have a field day when the customary bulwarks of conversation and dialogue are destroyed. The fresh perspective of an old friend has saved many a man from collapse at a point of crisis as he has had to face down fear and dread. In isolation there is little chance for that saving dialogue that redeems man from the panic of his own myopia.

An age longs for those things it lacks. Just as a hungry man speaks of food and a thirsty man dreams of drink, so modern man speaks of community, reconciliation, and openness. His yearnings bespeak his circumstances. In spite of, or perhaps because of, his technological togetherness, he is often lonely while in a crowd. His feasts have lost their festivity because his compassion has been professionalized and his concern institutionalized.

A dialogue is a discovery, for the heart of a dialogue is not merely information transmitted to another, it is the increasing awareness of another person and of oneself. A good conversation leads one into new insights about oneself, gleaned out of the fresh perspective of another. Many a man has gained new strength from the affirmation of an old friend in a time of trial. Many another man has been liberated from destructive illusions about himself by the biting judgments of either a friend or an enemy. A friendship which is only adulatory is finally demonic, for it maintains the illusions that insulate one from reality. A man never understands his masculinity alone but in terms of other men and women. During her years of maturation a young woman needs sound masculine relationships to understand her burgeoning womanhood. People understand themselves in relationship, not in isolation.

Whether deliberate torture or the by-product of a computerized society, isolation removes man from the strengths, resources, and insights of conversation and dialogue. He is left alone and without help. In his book *Shantung Compound,* Langdon Gilkey speaks very poignantly of his saving, strengthening, and liberating relationships during his internment by the Japanese in China during the Second World War. He remembers especially his warm friendship with Matthew and Edith Read, British Methodist missionaries from Tientsin. "Thus we were all delighted to find that invaluable addition to a quiet life: conversational partners with whom one's experiences can be shared and enriched. For through such conversations not only was I able to learn my own mind by talking out my thoughts; even more it was possible for me to see things anew through the wiser eyes of that unusual couple."[1]

The purpose of conversation with a trusted friend is to enjoy the presence of the other, not to gain or give information or to seek favors. In an age which supposedly values communication, the old delights and enjoyments of conversation have been lost. A bumper sticker may communicate an idea, but it offers no chance for dialogue, response, or insight. It cuts off dialogue while communicating.

The utility of communication has replaced the celebration of conversation in our day. An arid purposefulness has dried up the streams of dialogue. The purpose of communication is to impart information. Conversation, on the other hand, is a communion, a celebration of the presence of someone loved and trusted. Communication can take place by means of computers and print-outs. Dialogue can only take place with a person.

Once a utilitarian purpose is introduced into a celebration, the celebration soon goes by the board. The dissonant whine of an agenda, the cacophony of communication, destroys the harmonies, variations, and fugues of celebration. Nearly everyone has had the experience of a party gradually being muffled by a business partner talking shop or a mother criticizing the behavior of neighborhood children. The celebration dies because it is transformed into communication, sometimes with the best of intentions. The businessman may begin his destruction of the party by saying to himself, "This is the only chance I'll ever have to get at him."

There is indeed a time and place for communication, for imparting information, for persuading people, for selling services and ideas. When a man buys gasoline, he

1. Langdon Gilkey, *Shantung Compound* (New York: Harper and Row, 1966), p. 51.

is right to be interested in price and performance and not in a celebration of the presence of the top executive of the oil company. It is altogether healthy for a man to think impersonally in the areas of commerce, merchandising, politics, and manufacture, because he is after information, not presence. He should not really care what a salesman thinks of him, only if the salesman is communicating honestly.

A good bit of the obscenity of modern advertising rests in the confusion of communication with communion. One suspects that if a manufacturer does not wish to communicate because he has something to hide, then he introduces a cheap surrogate for communion — some female flesh, a famous personality, a few pleasing pictures of the countryside, even a child at play. Many people are taken in by this device, accepting the association of these surrogates with communion because they have never had the real thing.

Though the obscenity of advertising is objectionable, far more important to the lonely people of our modern civilization is the profound corruption of personal dialogue under the aegis of communication and utility. Just what good is this accomplishing? is the question raised by well-meaning harbingers of this corruption. This utilitarian attitude perhaps explains why modern man has so much trouble understanding worship, much less worshiping, for worship is not communication, propaganda, or sales. It is a communion with another, a celebration of the presence of Christ, just as dialogue is a celebration of the presence of someone loved. Once dialogue has an agenda it is no longer celebration and communion, merely communication. The frequency with which strangers indecently expose themselves emotionally to one another testifies to the lack of communion in the lives of many people today. A man with sound friendships is not likely to reveal himself willy-nilly to every passerby. It is the person who has not exposed himself in celebration to someone he loves who attempts to get the experience of communion by an artificial dialogue with those whom he neither knows nor trusts and therefore cannot love.

Dialogue takes place when two people enjoy each other and are free to reveal themselves in trust and love. It is never a matter of compulsion. Rather, it is a matter of expectancy, which may indeed become so strong that the times of relationship will achieve a certain regularity. If that regularity is confused with compulsion or obligation, however, then the vivacity of the dialogue is lost.

Augustine said that God made men for himself, and that men were restless until they rested in God. Just as men are made for relationship with each other, so they are made for relationship with God. They are incurably religious, though the religion may take some highly secular and unsatisfying forms. Man longs for things and relationships which he cannot touch and which do not perish.

Just as it is difficult to conceive of a full life spent in isolation, so it is difficult to conceive of such a life spent without dialogue. Some do choose to live without it, however, and they survive, in a minimal fashion. This decision merely to survive rather than to live may be rooted in a fear of exposure. Adam and Eve hid themselves in the foliage of the Garden of Eden so that the Lord God could not find them. Many people today spend their lives hiding behind various masks and roles, the foliage of social custom and usage.

The fear of exposure may be a product of that primal human fallacy, attempting to live without means of support. This drive for independence lay behind the fall of

Adam and Eve. They wanted to live without relying on anyone else, especially God. Ironically, their compulsion for freedom won them no freedom at all, only alienation and loneliness. Wishing to be free, they made their own prison, the prison of isolation. Adam and Eve are not historical characters. They are symbols for every man who has ever wanted to live the illusion that he could make it on his own.

The fundamental assumption behind the idea of a dialogue with God—commonly called prayer—is that one enjoys the presence of God. The Bible tells us that God delights in his creatures (Isa. 42:1). However, the church and much of popular piety as well have forgotten this with a misplaced concern for obligation. If a person does something out of obligation, the assumption is that he has yet to feel that it is a vital part of his own life. Guilt as a motivation for a dialogue with God does not produce a dialogue but a rote ritual whose only meaning is that it has been performed.

The rueful reality of the present life of the church is that prayer has little vital force. Many are baffled by it. They understand, on the one hand, that the official policy of the church pushes prayer as a good thing, but on the other hand they feel that it does not make much difference in their lives. It has come to seem like a polite ritual or a burdensome chore. With the possible exception of common worship, prayer has thus fallen into disuse. The sense of obligation that remains stems from the church's perception that a sense of the presence of God is vital to life itself. Unfortunately, making people feel obligated to pray will not solve the problem.

The issue is really very simple. Either prayer does not make any sense and should be discarded without much ado, or it has value and should be reevaluated in our modern era. If it has been of great value in the past, it may be merely the acids of modernity that have caused its neglect. Certainly there have been many misunderstandings and corruptions of prayer; if these could be overcome, modern man might find more of a place for it in his life.

Some would say that the disuse of prayer is due to the loss of a sense of transcendence, a sense of wonder and awe. This may be true in a very circumscribed area. The ability of a rationalistic civilization to come to terms with mystery and absurdity is notoriously limited, yet while the intellect of modern man has been hedged in, there has been a longing for something else. Much of the protest among the young has revolved around this point. They have often taken a rather ineffective romantic route, but their protest points to a sense of wonder that their predecessors lacked.

There have been two general sources of the misunderstanding of prayer: the official policy of the church and the popular understanding among many professing Christians. Officially, the church has taught that prayer is a means of grace, one of the channels by which God influences or infuses our lives. Popular piety has assumed that prayer, on the contrary, is one of the means by which man informs, influences, or persuades God. Both have introduced the machinery of communication into what was understood originally as a celebration of the presence of God.

The official policy has a faint taint of mechanism in its implication that a person who goes through the obligatory rituals will somehow receive a blessing. What this "blessing" might be has never been carefully spelled out, but that is not really the issue. Something that should be a celebration has been turned into a mechanistic obligation that is really but one-half of a transaction. The other half is the return blessing that man is supposed to get.

The popular position is far more personal, for it looks upon God as needing information and persuasion. If someone is sick, then the thing to do is to inform God of the sickness and persuade him to cure it. This can be done by pleading, coercion, or bargaining. God can be implored to remedy the sickness. He can be coerced by having "a great chain of prayer" which will impress him by the sheer weight of numbers. This is the "gang-up-on-God" theory of intercessory prayer. Finally, a bargain can be made in which one promises to do, or even to believe, certain things if only the sickness can be cured. The fact that this attitude is repugnant to the biblical faith (and even decency) has never seemed to still its force in popular piety.

Far outweighing the corruptions mentioned above has been a notion shared by both the official policy and popular piety, the notion that the presence of God is not a matter of enjoyment but of utility. According to this view, prayer has a purpose: it changes things. In official church policy it changed man, and in popular piety it changed God. Apparently, in all these comings and goings it was never seriously entertained that prayer is at heart a personal enjoyment of God's presence, a celebration of the relationship between God and man.

The impact of the mechanistic outlook of the official church position is that many of the common prayers of worship have become tedious. There is some justification for the accusation made by a certain type of virulent Protestant that these have become "canned prayers." At issue is not really the effectiveness of common prayer, however, but the lack of imagination and antiquated quality of much of the church's public worship.

The Christian faith is at heart a personal relationship between man and God in Jesus Christ, in the context of a community. Therefore, any attempt at understanding and practicing the art of prayer requires that a man know where he stands. The popular view of prayer at least has the virtue of seeing the personal element of prayer, but the possibility of a dialogue of discovery is rendered remote by its utilitarian attitude. Such an attitude inevitably means an abuse of dialogue, for a personal relationship in which communication and propaganda have replaced communion and celebration finally becomes unreal. The appearance of relationship may remain to deceive the unwary, but the substance gradually goes. Prayer is a dialogue of discovery, discovery which is the product of communion with a presence and celebration of a relationship.

The utilitarian attitude toward prayer is rooted partly in the presupposition that one resorts to prayer only when everything else has failed. Implicit in much of utilitarian prayer is the notion that God is a "god of the gaps" in human knowledge. When a man can no longer take care of his own problems, then he turns to God in prayer.

The understanding of prayer as a last resort undoubtedly is rooted in the understanding of faith as the leap taken when reason has reached the end of its tether. A man will go as far as his wits will carry him, and then he will go on through faith and prayer. Both faith and prayer are addenda to life rather than integral to it. This means that as knowledge increases and the gaps are filled, both faith and prayer become less important. This is what has happened in the modern era: knowledge and technology have increased, and faith and prayer have gradually fallen by the wayside.

The reevaluation and reconstruction of prayer must begin with the assumption made by the debonaire disciple, the assumption of God's graciousness in Jesus Christ. This graciousness has been given to man personally through the context of the community of faith, and the heart of man's relationship with God is the enjoyment of his gracious presence in a personal communion and celebration. The church has rightly understood prayer as the center of one's faithful experience. If the biblical faith is correct that God delights in his love for man, then it is altogether appropriate that man respond with an enjoyment and celebration of that love — not with a utilitarian agenda.

CHAPTER 8

THE DISCIPLINES OF ECSTASY

Every man has had the sickening experience of becoming aware that the initial friendliness of another person was merely an ingratiating ploy used to soften one up for the hard sell. The tender traps laid for us all have made most of us wary. There is a distinction between one old friend coming to another out of a need for help and someone *using* a friendship, and that distinction is one of the disciplines of ecstasy. Out of his loneliness every man must reach for a relationship, but once he *uses* that relationship it is damaged or destroyed. The first discipline of ecstasy is its uselessness. It has no utilitarian purpose.

Ecstasy is that absolutely necessary human experience in which a man stands outside himself and sees both himself and everyone and everything else in a new way. Some call it a vision, and others call it a dream, but if a man lives without it, he is less than a man. Ecstasy can lead one man to say to another, "I need you"; without ecstasy he is liable to think, "I want to use you."

Prayer becomes difficult when it is thought to have a purpose and is thus made into a matter of work rather than play. Play is useless. It serves no utilitarian purpose. It is a small form of ecstasy, for it allows a man to stand outside himself, even if only for a brief period. He forgets himself because he is having such a good time. Play is not frivolous, however; it stands at the very heart of human life. Without it a man is a drudge. With it he has the makings of a human being. Unlike play, work is something a man does to accomplish a purpose. It is utilitarian. One might suppose that the happiest of all men are those whose ostensible work is really their play, and the most miserable of all men are those whose ostensible play is still their work. The latter can never let go. They are always at it.

A good relationship, although useless, is not happenstance. One of the gravest errors made by many who believe that the heart of life is play is drawing the conclusion that play is without discipline. Ecstasy does not happen by chance. It happens when people are ready for it, and getting ready for it is the discipline of ecstasy. Just as good play requires that there be rules of the game, so the dialogues of discovery require the disciplines of ecstasy.

One often hears people say that they only pray when they feel like it, in the mistaken belief that "feeling like it" is necessary for sincerity. A person's emotional state at any given time is not the basis of a relationship, however; emotions are the products of a relationship, not the cause of it. One of the first disciplines of ecstasy is establishing a continuity of relationship, a regularity of association. Once a wife talks to her husband only when she feels like it, the marriage is in for trouble. A good relationship requires regular periods, times, and moments when people exchange the symbols of love.

Sincerity of relationship does not depend upon depth of feeling but upon degree of commitment. It hangs upon one's will, not one's emotions. The relationship is a product of a decision, and the emotions it involves are also a product of that decision. Anger is as much a legitimate emotion of a deep relationship as is pleasure; both feelings cannot help but arise in the context of a strong and sincere caring. Conversely, if a person does not care, he is likely to have little emotion of any sort.

Feelings of pleasure and gratification are more likely to predominate in a relationship if it has some continuity, if there are regular times, periods, and occasions of exchange. If continuity is thus one of the disciplines of ecstasy, one of the things which prepare us for moments of insight, then some continuity would seem essential for the dialogue of discovery with God. Often little of importance is communicated during these regular times of relationship, but they establish a pattern which is vital to the maintenance and growth of the relationship.

Not only are continuity and regularity important, but so are the social amenities. In an age as crass as ours, the thought of propriety and courtesy seems almost antiquated. However, the lackluster times do not lessen the necessity of amenities. Thanking one's wife for a dinner well prepared and served, thanking children for a job well done, thanking friends for acts of generosity — all are out of favor in a thankless age but still essential to sound relationships. One does not have to feel deeply to be grateful, and a repetitive act of courtesy is not needfully perfunctory. While civility may be out of fashion, it is still essential.

An ecstatic occasion is far more likely to occur in the dialogue of discovery with God if the disciplines of that ecstasy have been carefully nurtured. If a man regularly thanks God for his meat, he is far more likely to feel that he lives in the presence of God. A man who customarily thanks his wife for symbols of her love is much more likely to live in the presence of her love. Courtesies and amenities are systems of symbols that enliven and strengthen a relationship, and without them the relationship suffers. A relationship may survive crassness, but it will never grow because of it.

One of the difficulties of modern man is that he wants to get over the preliminaries, thinking that they are merely impediments when in fact they are really avenues. Thanking God for food before eating is not ecstasy, and doing it every time one eats is not a dialogue of discovery. However, the system of relationship created by such regular acts of courtesy produces the atmosphere in which that ecstasy will occur. The ancient insistence upon regular times of prayer was not misplaced. What was misplaced was the sense of routine obligation.

A system of relationship will have some effectiveness only if the relationship is first of all a matter of enjoyment. The enjoyment and celebration of God's gracious presence in our lives is the basis of the dialogue of discovery, not the system of relationship. There must be — not out of obligation but out of joy — regular times which a man sets aside to enjoy the presence of God.

Within the context of the tradition of faith certain elements of this dialogue of discovery have been seriously misunderstood. Certainly, into any good relationship a man brings himself, just as he is, without pretense or agenda. A dialogue of discovery cannot take place if one is afraid to reveal oneself. The root of ecstasy is the faithful conviction that in spite of everything God is graciously disposed toward man.

Misunderstandings have arisen, however, out of a mechanistic view of prayer in which a person approaches God with his agenda, sometimes out of fear, often merely with the thought of unburdening himself or asking for something. Prayer is not a spigot which allows a man to turn the divine presence on or off. It is a relationship in which one enjoys the presence of God. If this is the case, does asking God for anything have any place in prayer? The answer lies in the distinction between needing God and using him, and that distinction is found in the attitude of the one praying.

In prayer, as in any vital relationship, there is always

a self-revelation. A husband may understand his wife's needs before she expresses them, but it is essential to the relationship that they be expressed and worked out, as it were. The dialogue of discovery takes place when a man sees himself in terms of his own interpretations of his needs in relationship to another who is graciously disposed toward him. Sometimes a man inchoately senses a need but defines it poorly. A desire for importance is a legitimate desire, but the forms it takes are often destructive. A man may make a fool of himself so that people will notice him, forsaking a more tedious but more constructive means of doing something worthwhile. One of the fruits of a dialogue of discovery is that in an atmosphere of graciousness a man may be liberated from his folly and thus freed to do something really important.

So unburdening ourselves to God in prayer is necessary, for in seeing our needs in relationship to someone else we see ourselves in a new way. However, the problem remains of the place of asking God for things, attitudes, and answers. At first sight, a mechanistic and utilitarian prayer would seem the only context in which a person could pray for a sick friend, for his own health, for wisdom in rearing children, and for enlightenment in the problems of marriage. It is something like going to the "answer man," paying your money, and getting the answer.

However, this attitude toward prayer leaves something out, that which a very fine physician lacks if he is a cold fish. Many people leave a doctor's office unsatisfied, for while they got excellent technical advice and treatment, they sensed, rightly or wrongly, that the doctor really did not care. Asking for help from a friend is a far cry from using that friend to gain something. The distinction is in the attitude. Using someone to get something is not the same thing as turning to someone loved out of a deeply felt need. It is the distinction between communication and communion, utility and relationship.

The saying "prayer changes things" is true only when prayer is not *used* to change things, for the change takes place only as a gift, not by intention. A marriage is doomed to trivial animosity if the wife begins it with a campaign of reformation, for rather than establishing a relationship, she will achieve at best a sullen manipulation. Both men and women change in marriage, but the change is not by design. It is the fruit of a relationship.

When a man prays his concerns, they can only be set in the context of a communion. God is not ignorant, malevolent, or indifferent. He knows before we ask, and thus when we lay our concerns, anxieties, and needs before him, it is not with the intent of informing him or persuading him. It is the revelation of ourselves. It is the openness of any good relationship.

We cannot know whether or not God is changed by prayer, but we might suspect that if God's relationship with men is steadfast, he will adjust in the way he relates to man as man changes. If a father's graciousness is constant, the way he relates to his child will change as the child moves from infancy to adolescence and on to maturity. This transformation in the style of the relationship is possible only if both parties accept the change. Many a mother would like to see her son grow up, but the son prefers to remain tied to her apron strings.

A good relationship is a changing relationship, and the chances of transformation are much higher if it is based in some regularity of association. The traditional way to insure regularity in man's relationship with God was generally by means of morning and evening prayers, often on the knees. That style may suit some, but because it suits some does not make it universally valid. There are no sacred times, places, or postures. For some praying on their knees at the crack of dawn may fit. For others sitting in an easy chair with a glass of wine may fit. If the relationship is to be vital and transforming, then regularity is fundamental, but the style of that regularity is a matter of taste.

For a great many people prayer is a wordy affair in which the chief activity appears to be a verbal bombardment of God. God does all the listening and man all the speaking. This is not a dialogue but an unsatisfying monologue. The problem is very simple. God is not given a chance to speak or to make his presence known, and therefore prayer becomes communication rather than communion. Communion is the enjoyment and celebration of a presence. It may involve some communication, but communication is not the heart of it. If prayer is fundamentally a communion with God, then words are important to it, but they are not its heart.

One does not conjure up God by prayer; he is always present in a man's life. Rather, through prayer a person becomes aware of a presence that is always there. The dialogue of discovery is thus not essentially a matter of verbal communication but of awareness of the presence of God and of the meaning of that presence in one's life. This awareness depends upon contemplation—of the meaning of the gospel, of Scripture, of important Christian thought. In other words, it requires a time of relative quiet when one can think about the meaning of the presence of God.

Some people raise questions about prayer because they recognize that in a relationship with another person they can hear and see the other person, while in prayer the dialogue appears to be carried on in isolation. This observation is disturbing until one thinks carefully about how one senses the presence of others. It is really an inner matter. Some people can do a great deal of talking and still one does not really sense their presence. Others are relatively quiet and their presence is strongly sensed. Indeed, many times the blind can sense a situation with greater power than those who can see. The ability to sense the presence of another is not merely a matter of the five senses, for it rests on what the heart and mind of a person do with data received from his senses. In silence and darkness one can be acutely aware of another. A great deal of this awareness depends upon one's memory of past experiences of presence.

Given the suggestion above that prayer is communion, not communication, some will ask, "Does praying for a sick child do any good, then?" The answer depends on what is meant. If the question refers to an improvement in the child's chances of getting well, then one must reply that we do not finally know. But if it refers to an increased openness to God's movements in our anxieties, then the answer is a simple yes. It is possible that the healing powers of God's graciousness might be opened up through a change on the part of man as a result of his relationship with God. The channels of God's love to man are men, and the problem is not God, but man. The hope of men rests in a change, not in God, but in men.

The important matter in prayer, then, is not changing God through persuasion, coercion, or bargaining. It is the celebration of his presence in a personal communion. The distinction between a man of peace praying for peace and a man of hostility praying for peace is an unseen distinction of attitude. One is coming to a relationship with his concerns in the context of a communion. The other is using and therefore abusing a relationship. If even the simplest men are hard to deceive on this score, it would seem likely that God is not much fooled either. If prayer is not at heart a means of enhancing a relationship, it reverts quite quickly to a mechanistic attitude.

Rather than thinking of prayer as a means or channel of grace or as a device to get something we want, we should think of it as a personal response to the immediacy of God's grace in life. It is not so much a laying of our desires as a laying of ourselves before him. It is not so much an obligation as a grateful and joyous response to a gracious stimulus. The assumption is that God knows and cares, and the problem is not so much how to influence him as it is how to understand oneself in terms of his gracious initiative.

Many of the current social crises stem from the fact that we live in a society which is impersonal — even antipersonal — competitive, and achievement-oriented. Only confusion and chaos can result from people trying to understand themselves amidst impersonal behemoths while competing against indifferent abstractions. The sad thing is that man understands himself finally in dialogue, but in today's world there is precious little with which one might have a dialogue. How does one understand himself as a student in dialogue with abstractions like grades given to him on IBM cards? How does a man understand himself, much less his work, when it is impossible for him to know the whole of his work or the people who conceived it?

Prayer is essentially a dialogue with God in which a man understands himself finally in terms of God himself and his graciousness toward man. The revelation of God in Jesus Christ, as William Temple noted, is not information about God but the disclosure of God himself. From this disclosure of God himself man is able through the dialogue of prayer to understand himself.

In the beginning of the *Institutes,* Calvin said that human wisdom consists in the knowledge of God and the knowledge of man, and then he raised the question as to which of these is prior. He concluded that the knowledge of God is prior, be that knowledge ever so slight. He went on to say, "It is certain that man never achieves a clear knowledge of himself unless he has first looked upon God's face."[1]

Calvin was saying that man finally understands himself through a dialogue with God, and thus prayer is not so much a mechanical series of petitions as it is an immediate, personal encounter with God through which man understands himself. If a man is to understand and accept himself, he must measure himself. In today's world he is offered only the opportunity of an impersonal, abstract, indifferent, and electronic measurement. Through the dialogue of prayer a man measures himself in terms of God's graciousness initiated in Jesus Christ.

The current abstractionism and impersonalism make two traditional functions of the church especially important. One is the fellowship of the community as symbolized in the Lord's Supper, and the other is prayer. Prayer is not obligatory if one is to merit God's graciousness, but it is at the heart of being a human being. It is basically an enjoyment of—even a basking in—God's mercy. It is living with the assumption of the ultimacy of love. It is the immediate perception that behind and amidst all the ambiguity and absurdity of life the fundamental reality of life is love.

When our Lord enjoined us to pray without ceasing, he was obviously referring to a style of life, a sense of the immediacy and intimacy of God's graciousness to man. Those who "pray without ceasing" have the easy and quiet confidence about life which stems from a sense of God's gracious presence.

1. John Calvin, *The Institutes of the Christian Religion,* ed. John T. McNeill, trans. Ford Lewis Battles, 2 vols., The Library of Christian Classics, vols. 20–21 (Philadelphia: Westminster Press, 1960), 1:37.

CHAPTER 9

A QUESTIONABLE FAITH

Looking at something upside down may be a good way of gaining a fresh perspective of it. This is especially the case if looking at it right side up has not been working too well. For many people Christian doctrine has not been too pleasant a sight right side up. For one thing, it is usually as dry as dust. It often answers questions no one in several millennia has bothered to ask. Many times it seems like something written by men with chastity belts on their imaginations and senses of humor. It may be time to look at Christian doctrine upside down, as a series of questions rather than as a series of answers.

Much of dogma and creed seems like the product of people who really did not want to come to terms with the risks of faith and chose the securities of dogma as a cheap substitute. Dietrich Bonhoeffer wrote of a hypocritical piety which spoke of the necessity of faith but which was in fact practical atheism: while mouthing platitudes about God, it attempted to live as if God were not. He called it *securitas*, living without the risks and demands of faith.[1]

The three areas of our experience in which we usually find examples of *securitas* are the mind, the emotions, and morals. It is a very easy thing indeed for a man to substitute words for experience. It is far less demanding

1. Dietrich Bonhoeffer, *Temptation*, trans. Kathleen Downham (London: SCM Press, 1955), pp. 41 f.

an activity to postulate theories of compassion than to
be compassionate. A great many parents lamentably are
adept at spinning off hypotheses about child rearing
while sending their children away for an entire summer
at camp. The word is not the thing. It is a witness to it.
It is easier to witness to a thing than to be a part of it.

The effect of this attitude is that doctrines become
surrogates for experience. Many so-called believers are
strong on doctrine and weak on faith. Indeed, the more
they become fascinated with doctrine, the more insistent
they become that their doctrinal scheme is the final answer. They seek a creedal *securitas* impregnable to the
assault of God's presence. If a person once thinks that
he has the answers, then he need no longer place his
trust in anyone, not even God. He has an effective
substitute for faith as long as he can live in his card-
board world.

In addition to using mental straitjackets as substitutes
for faith, there are many who would make feelings a
surrogate for experiences. Among the avant-garde of
modern American culture this is the most prevalent
substitute. When one is more likely to be asked what he
feels about an issue than what he thinks about it, one
knows that he has left the age of reason and entered the
age of feeling. Having been enjoined to deal with "guilt
feelings" rather than with guilt, many modern men have
concluded that feeling is the reality of life. Deep feeling
becomes a substitute for clear thinking.

Feeling can just as readily be a surrogate for experience as thinking. Just as genuine and creative thought
is devastated by a rigid dogmatism, so real emotion is
laid waste by the sentimentalism of an emotional idola-
try. Emotions are a part of a person's response to an
experience, but without the experience they are morbid.
Distaste and dislike may accompany a strong com-

mitment to a cause or a person; along with these feelings there may also be liking, delight, and even reverence. A man's emotional response to his wife will change, but his relationship to her and his commitment to her will not have varied. The emotional intensity of a given occasion will reflect his own emotional needs as well as the significance of the relationship.

Under the pressure of the group misguided people often generate an emotional state which they deem to be the experience of religious conversion. Indeed, many people have come to think of conversion as merely an adolescent emotional upheaval. There is more to it than that, however. A true conversion is likely to take place when a man has come to the end of the road in terms of his life's meaning. The system of values that has been guiding him gradually fails to give substance or hope to his existence. His world begins to fall apart. The loss of a job by an advocate of the work ethic, the toll of the years on an aging beauty queen, the realization that too many relationships have gone sour—these are the types of experiences that lead a person to a decisive change. Conversion is such a change in which a person finds his final source of meaning in the person of Jesus Christ.

It is natural and wholesome for such a change to involve significant emotional responses, but they are not the change. They are the results and products of the change. Not infrequently a person who is unwilling to face the profound malaise of his life will seek a way out through an emotional substitution for such a change. That is really nothing more than a religious autoeroticism in which one substitutes self-induced fancies for a genuine experience.

The current rage for emotional involvement can be a sickness in which one attempts to escape life by faking it with feelings. Deep feelings can be as much a *securitas* as right thought, for they can be a means by which one avoids faith. The self-induced emotional upheaval of pseudoconversion and the sentimentalities of syrupy religious art are not the same thing as faith, for faith is that profound experience in which a man becomes aware that he no longer lives by his own surrogates for experience, that is to say, by his own strength, but rather in the context of God's graciousness in Jesus Christ.

In addition to thought and emotion, many have used morals as a substitute for faith. In the popular imagination "being good" has about the same meaning as "being Christian." A believer is one who behaves himself. If a person could ape the ethics of the Christian, he might not in his own mind be forced to go through the rigors of the Christian experience. He could build a *securitas* of goodness and render himself immune to faith by morals.

Morals are significant, but if they become a substitute for experience, they can become diabolical. Many marriages endure for years on the basis of a carefully observed propriety which is really the means by which the people avoid a direct experience of each other. So "the Christian way of life" has as often as not become a means by which one could avoid the immediate experience of God's grace in Jesus Christ. Morals then become burdens to be borne rather than means of expressing a new life. The risk of being born again into a new life is too much for many, and they lamentably prefer the fetters of secondhand morals over the ethical adventure of new life.

The matter that concerns us the most here is the issue of thinking as a Christian. Is the aim "right thought" or "clear thinking"? If it is right thought, then one is at a dead end, faced with submission to a tyranny in which someone else determines what is in fact "right thought." If it is clear thinking, than one is beginning a venture in increasing understanding.

Christian thought is not a disinterested investigation

into religion. It is an attempt to give clarity and understanding to religious experience. As such, it can only occur after the experience. There are some souls who like to arrive at a finished theory before they put themselves into something. They read all manner of books on child rearing before having the child, unaware that the books only make sense after one has had the child. Many churches are burdened with theoretical specialists on parish life who have never had a satisfactory parish experience. Thought about something can only occur after that something has been experienced. To be sure, one can entertain some preliminary observations, but they are only that and should be given only slight attention. In the end, theory succeeds experience; it does not precede it.

Theology is the attempt to understand what has in fact happened. "Theology may be defined as the study which, through participation in, and reflection upon a religious experience, seeks to express the content of this faith in the clearest and most coherent language possible."[2] Such an activity is valuable because it gives the experience a fuller meaning and enables one to communicate one's faith more effectively. A questionable faith is one in which the reality is the faith, and the thinking is the constant questioning and probing that goes on in finding out what the faith means. Theology is thus not a series of final answers to questions no one is asking. It is a series of probing questions about the nature of the religious experience. The educated man is the man who asks the right questions, not the one who knows the right answers. Answers are the end of thinking, questions the beginning.

Frequently one sees bumper stickers with the slogan Christ Is the Answer. He is also the question, because

2. John Macquarrie, *Principles of Christian Theology* (New York: Charles Scribner's Sons, 1966), p. 1.

once he has encountered a man, that man has a whole new series of questions about himself and life which will remain with him as long as he lives. If he thinks he possesses the final answers to those questions, he will become a case of arrested development. For most people the creeds and dogmas of the church have been such an end to inquiry, for they have been seen as a series of answers. In fact, they can be seen as a series of questions about the experience of God's graciousness in Christ, questions which the church puts to every man claiming that experience. A significant part of education is the awareness that there are profound questions that one has never thought of by oneself, or that one has thought of but would just as soon avoid. The creeds are the attempt of the church to lead believers beyond pleasant and self-indulgent questions to demanding and growing ones.

The doctrine of the Trinity actually does not say much about God at all. In reality it is not an abstract speculation about the nature of God but a series of profound questions about the unity and diversity of one's experience of God. God reveals himself in many different ways. He is at once near and far, judging and forgiving, demanding and encouraging. The question put to the believer is less about God himself than about the ways in which he encounters man. The question of the Trinity probes a man to think beyond a simple experience to a multifaceted one, and to think of an essential unity amidst that diversity.

The tragedy of the wrong question is that it always leads to an ineffective answer. Those who seek a simple answer to questions about God's nature are asking a wrong question which leads to an elimination of real experiences because they fail to fit into a system in which unity means uniformity. If God is love, then any experience that does not fit the prevailing idea of love is not a real experience of God. Many times the liberals in theology have been the most severely restrictive in this respect, holding that an experience is wrong if it does not fit their self-styled "enlightened theology."

The unity and diversity of God are problems for a man only after the diversity of God has encroached on his life. The fearful God who commanded the forces of nature in creation is also the God who bled for him as a Savior and who infuses his life with vitality as the Spirit. Is the God whom one experiences as an unfathomable and awesome Creator when surveying the midnight skies the same God who died on the cross and who abides with us in our loneliness? The Trinity is a series of thoughtful questions put to a believer when he finally understands that the dark night of his soul is really the shadow of God's hand.

Theology has but one function, the illumination of our experience as human beings. If it does not do that, then it is useless. In its traditional forms it has often confused and baffled believers. It has been taught as a series of dry-as-dust abstractions that had little to do with the business of living. Indeed, it was more often than not used as a means of escaping life. Its true purpose is to illuminate life. It is not a lot of theoretical questions about the nature of God. It is rather about God's relationship with man.

In the third chapter of Exodus it is reported that God called an unlikely candidate to lead the people of Israel out of Egypt. Moses tried to avoid that relationship by asking an abstract question about God. When he asked for God's name, in ancient Semitic culture he was really asking what God was like. For his pains he got the delightfully obscure reply, "I am who I am," which on reflection says nothing at all. The real issue that Moses had to face was God's demand, not some abstraction about his nature.

The creeds and dogmas of the church have as often as not been fetters of the mind. They ought to be guides and probes encouraging the debonaire disciple to grow beyond himself. It is important that a person understand himself, not only in terms of his present interpretations but also in terms of new ones made possible by questions he has yet to ask. Theology is that disciplined questioning that moves a man to new understandings of his life, not because someone has told him its meaning, but because he has discovered it for himself in the school of faith.

As we have seen, the relationship of the Bible to a man's development in faith is one of the crucial issues. The Bible is a human document, and any avoidance of that central reality is going to lead one down the wrong path. It is the grappling by the community of faith with the great events in human history by which God revealed himself. As with all human attempts to understand what God has in fact done, God is there himself, helping man to understand. When one speaks of the inspiration of the Bible, one is saying that when man attempts to understand his relationship to God, God does not leave man bereft of his presence to find it out all by himself.

Each major creed within the Christian church arose at a time when the faith was being threatened by destructive questions; the creed was the church's attempt to set more constructive questions. For instance, there have been many attempts to ask questions about the nature of Jesus in such a way that only one answer is possible. You don't really believe that Jesus is the Son of God, do you? is in fact a statement in the form of a question. The early creeds of the church were all written in response to such issues.

The authority of the Bible for the believer rests in the view that the Bible is really the creed of creeds. It was the beginning of the whole process by which men have attempted to understand God's ways with men, with his help. All of theology is really but a footnote to the Bible.

The Bible gains authority only when one has experienced the reality to which it bears witness. Without faith the Bible is just another historical curiosity, but with faith it is the primal document that leads a man in thinking out the meaning of his experience. Happily the Bible does not present just one set of questions and answers, for it was written by different men at different times. Each one looked at the central events of God's revelation through the prism of his own peculiar set of circumstances. Paul's understanding of the Christian faith is not exactly the same as John's. The Gospel of Matthew looks at things differently than that of Luke. All of these interpretations point to the same fundamental experience of graciousness in Jesus Christ, but they do so with a wondrous variety. This variety illuminates our experience today, opening up many avenues of understanding.

The faith of the debonaire disciple is questionable not because it is unsteady and uncertain but because of its confidence in the grace of God in Jesus Christ. This confidence is borne out in the Bible, a book that could include a Matthew who saw in Jesus a new and greater Moses, a John who saw Jesus as a light shining in the darkness, and a Paul who saw him as a justifier and reconciler. Great questions lead to a variety of answers. The Bible, the creeds, and the dogmas of the church offer those questions that lead a man beyond a party-line answer to new insights, insights which make the faith a fuller and more exciting adventure than living securely with someone else's answers to outdated questions. The task of theology is to illuminate the meaning of what has already happened to the believer in Jesus Christ.

CHAPTER 10

ENDURING AND PREVAILING

If humor is a prelude to faith, no adequate grasp of the life of the debonaire disciple can leave the matter of faith unattended. Humor deals with the preliminaries of life. Faith deals with the finalities. The incongruity which is the assumption of humor becomes a tragedy when written large. A boy tumbling off his bike may appear funny if he isn't hurt, but if he suffers brain damage, one has moved from humor to faith, for one has moved from incongruity to tragedy.

Tragedy is the central fact of human experience, and any view of life must come to terms with that brute fact. Indeed, much of human effort is spent in avoiding it. Burial grounds called memorial parks, whole subcultures devoted to sexual stimulation, movements nourished on the synthetic ecstasies of self-indulgence are prime examples of a culture trying to put an adhesive plaster on the sore wounds of man.

The conclusive and concluding tragedy which all men face is death, for it wipes away all that for which men live. If a man has given himself over to possessions, they do not endure. If he has found his meaning in relationships, they are lost. No matter what he values, it does not count in the end. One is apt to end with the gentle cynicism of Ecclesiastes: "This too is emptiness and chasing the wind" (2:26 NEB).

In addition to the brute fact of death, each man faces a series of little deaths for most of his life. The loss of an old friend, the ruin of a job, the waywardness of a child, the stupidity of parents—all are small forms of death in which a man's psychic supports are gradually eroded. The difficulty with these smaller serial calamities is that they cannot often be put in a reasonable framework.

For many faith is a means of finding life's answers, but the pathos is that so much of life is unanswerable. It is only in such things as fixing a radiator, roasting a leg of lamb, or getting the assignment correct that one can find answers to his questions. Even then it is often difficult. In the things that affect our lives, like the souring relationship with an old friend, the hostility and indifference of a child, the feelings of exhaustion and dejection after a success, finding an answer is seldom possible. Faith, then, is not so much the ability to find answers to the questions posed by life as it is the gift of living graciously and convivially without answers. Faith is the quality of life that gives a man the capacity to keep going, to endure and prevail, when all the answers have run out and the questions still abide.

In response to a tragedy, a man can ask one of two possible questions. He can ask why it happened, and he can ask how one can live within its context. The answers to the first question are always partial and limited. One can come to terms in some way with personal failures. If a man gets himself fired, if a woman makes a mess of a relationship, with some astute help they can learn and grow by asking themselves why they failed. They were in part responsible for the debacle, so they can perceive its meaning and may learn something from it. A good bit of life is filled with such problems, and the grace required honestly to face one's foibles under pressure is a quality not in the possession of many.

Most people avoid facing their failures squarely because they lack the quality of the debonaire disciple which allows him to continue to think well of himself even when he has made a mess of things. The vitality of his meaning is not tied to each little success and failure. It comes from the context of God's graciousness in Jesus Christ. If God is still hanging in there with him, then he can face his failures graciously, for his identity does not stand or fall with these failures but in God's grace.

Enduring and prevailing have to do with the events which confound us as well as with those we can understand. While one may learn and grow from a realization of the consequences of his own foibles, what does one do when a child is stricken with leukemia, a husband disintegrates, a wife and mother dies, a bomb drops? Events such as these are fundamentally without meaning. There is no way in which a rationale can be imposed upon them, and there is no way that one can learn through them to remedy the foibles that caused the tragedy.

For most men meaning comes from understanding the relationship between things. When one finds the causes of an event, he is liable to think he understands its meaning; when he can't, he is liable to think that the event is meaningless. Within these terms most of the things that overtake a man are meaningless. A young man may die in a war, and his parents think that his death had some meaning in that the boy gave his life for the cause of freedom. In retrospect, many view the war as an absurdity that need not have come to pass except for the foibles of politicians.

For the debonaire disciple courage is not rooted in rationality, for the center of his faith is found in the crucifixion and resurrection of Jesus Christ, an event which does not have a rational meaning. Looking at a mired humanity, we can find no reason to believe that this mass was worth the death of God's Son. It makes no sense. The genius of the debonaire disciple is that in the face of absurdity he takes courage. His question of why things overtake him is not answered. His question of how to live with courage and hope in the midst of them is. His faith is the root of his ability to live without answers to questions that never stop.

"Take up your cross and follow me" is not a call to some self-indulgent masochism that passes for Christian faith. It is a call to understand the tragedies of life in the context of God's tragedy for man. A woman can live with many unnerving faults in a man because she knows that there is something more to him, something that others cannot see. She has, as it were, the eyes of faith. The cross is not an answer to the speculative question as to why men suffer unjustly. It is rather God's participation in our suffering, and in that participation a man of faith sees that there is more to life than suffering. He is enabled to see beyond the nonsense and the tragedies to the core of human existence, the graciousness of God in the coming of Jesus Christ.

The meaning of an event is not found in one's analysis of it or in a discovery of its causation. It is found in one's participation in it. The physician may be able to explain the dynamics of cancer to the parents of a teenager stricken with the illness. He can speak knowledgeably about chemical treatments and cobalt therapy. His remarks contribute knowledge of the causes and effects of the situation, but the knowledge in no way relates to the parents' grief. The how of a tragic event gives it little meaning, if any, and seldom can one gain anything from the why of it. The matter rests in working through the event. The death of a small boy will either bring the parents closer together or it will drive them apart. The latter will happen if they do not both participate in the grief. The redemptive quality of their suffering will be the experience of grace when they find that they cannot stand alone. In finding each other, they will ultimately find the source of their graciousness, Jesus Christ.

The experiences that confound us drive us either to defiance or to a realization that we do not stand alone. A man will either lift up a clenched fist or drop to his knees in prayer. The cross of Jesus Christ is a paradigm for all the suffering of mankind, for just as God's graciousness was finally and conclusively present in that agony, so he is present in all agony. In his incarnation in Jesus Christ God placed himself on the block of human experience. He is not a remote and absolute deity unconnected with that experience. He has been and remains where man lives, in both the triumphs and the tragedies. The cross is the final declaration in deed of God's participation in the whole of human experience, and for this reason a man in his own tragedies is able to experience the graciousness of God.

The meaning of the cross, then, is found in a person's full participation in life with its triumphs and tragedies, and the courage for this participation comes from the sure and certain knowledge that God is there tending his own. Too often in the church the life of the cross has meant the indulgence of a masochistic desire to bolster one's ego through self-centered suffering. Taking up the cross is not courting tragedy. It is the ability to endure it and to prevail, not because one has found out why, but because one has found out how. The how lies in the awareness that something else is always there, something else which is really someone else, Jesus Christ.

The debonaire disciple is one who is free of care. That does not mean being careless but careful, for much of life's richness comes from the relationships that one assumes. When a child is born, the parents are assuming cares. They are willing to do so because of the vitality of their relationship with their children. The quality of their caring will be much more creative and rewarding if it is not a burden to be borne but a gift to be enjoyed. Almost any human relationship partakes of this elemental reality. Every vital human encounter costs a person something; the only way to avoid much of the suffering of life is to avoid life itself by avoiding relationships.

Often a young girl attempts to flee the problems of her home by escaping into marriage, only to find that marriage is more demanding than her home life was. Love is that quality of life which enables one to pay the price of relationships—and there is no relationship possible which does not have a price. Sometimes the qualities that one most admires in another will be the very qualities that cause the most pain. Parents will want their children to develop their own personalities and responsibilities, but in that development the children will grow away from dependence on their parents. A certain childlike closeness will be lost in the process of maturation, and the very thing admired will be the cause of the loss.

If a person could imagine for a moment a world in which cruelty and harshness were not only present but also believed to be the heart of life, he would see that when harshness and cruelty occurred in such a world, no one would think anything about it. If murder were an accepted method for the resolution of disputes, then a murder would not bother anyone. The thing that distresses people about murder is that although it is actually a part of life, it is unacceptable. A society is in trouble when the citizens are no longer indignant and aroused over mayhem and destruction. When a person can walk by degradation without flinching, he has witnessed to his own loss of principle. Indignation and outrage at suffering are testimonies to an ideal and a hope. Tragedy occurs when the brute events of life betray and deny that hope.

The business of living itself finally leads one to the necessity of tragedy, for all relationships run the risk of some type of destruction. There would be no widows if there were no marriages. There would be no bereaved parents if there were not first delighted parents. Tragedy can only occur if there was something precious that was either lost or damaged. Oddly enough, the destructive elements of human existence presuppose the goodness of the creation. The extent of grief is measured by the depth of the loss, and the depth of the loss is the measure of the original gift.

In a paradoxical way the grief and agony of life bear witness to its goodness, to the goodness of God's creation. If life were essentially ambiguous, then tragedy would be in the order of things, but the thing about tragedy is that it doesn't fit. It is an absurdity. If the world were morally indifferent, if truth, beauty, and goodness didn't count, then the lack of them or even their denial would not be tragic. The tragic occurs when men know that there is more to life than the mess they're in. The suffering of Jesus Christ on the cross is God's testimony to the original goodness of life, for in the cross the Savior is also the Creator, the one who made the midnight blue skies is also the one bleeding red.

Tragedy leads one inevitably to the question of why. Although that question can never be answered with satisfaction, it is itself a prelude to faith. The question assumes that there is something more than the tragedy itself. If the grinding poverty of the ghetto dweller is "just not right," then one presupposes that there is something else in life. Just as the wife with the odd husband endures his oddities and prevails over them because she knows that there is something more to the man, so the debonaire disciple endures and prevails because he, too, knows that there is more to life than tragedy. That something more was shown right in the midst of the tragedy of life, for God chose the cross to reveal his grace. That is right where the debonaire disciple begins, at the cross.

The carefree quality of the life of the debonaire disciple presupposes an enormous price. Every good quality in life calls for a sacrifice. When people go through life burdened by guilt or anxiety, they are trying to take the easy way out. The way out of guilt is forgiveness, and one of the most difficult things for a man to do is to accept forgiveness. He loses his independence and illusion of goodness by doing so, and for most people in their false pride, that is an enormous price. But it has to be paid to be carefree.

The graciousness of God is free, but it is never received without cost or given without cost. The cross of Jesus Christ is the cost of the gift, and that cost is the presupposition of the carefree life. This is why the debonaire disciple begins at the cross. If he begins there, he knows that there is no easy way out of his malaise. He must give it all up and let God claim him in faith.

In 1949 William Faulkner received the Nobel Prize for literature. In his acceptance speech before the Swedish Academy, he said that man would not only endure; he would also prevail. Too many men are content merely to endure, when in fact the heart of life is prevailing. The debonaire disciple in the midst of tragedy was best described by Paul, when he spoke of being more than conquerors. He had in mind the courage by which a man not only endures but also prevails. This courage comes not because he is strong but because he is faithful, for the source of his courage is in the love of God in Jesus Christ. He is so carefree that he can afford to be full of care, not full of cares.

CHAPTER 11

THE CONVIVIAL COMPANY

One of the splendid vices of American civilization is the old goal of "making it on my own." The theme behind this folk mythology is a spiritual atomism. Each man is a discrete, separate entity, sufficient unto himself. He is like a gyroscope spinning through life independent and unrelated. If he does have any ties, they are not indigenous. He needs no one because he can do it all by himself.

The avant-garde of modern civilization thinks that this gyroscopic personality is a relic out of the past, for modern therapeutic man supposedly believes in community. He attacks the individualistic Protestant work ethic and proclaims his identity with the struggling masses. He is strong on "group therapy" but at the same time likes to "do his own thing." He spends a great deal of time "trying to get it all together" in "group think" sessions.

Being strong on "deep relationships" he ironically also believes in divorce. Apparently he operates on the peculiar conviction that one can move in and out of deep relationships at one's convenience. Indeed, some espouse the theory that marriage is irrelevant because it makes too many demands and is broken only with difficulty. They believe in a relationship and a community without a commitment transcending tomorrow's displeasure and annoyance.

Endemic to both the supporters of the old Protestant work ethic and the modern flimflam therapeutic man is a fatal flaw, the flaw of atomism. When the Bible spoke of every man doing what was right in his own sight, it was leveling a condemnation against Israel because the people no longer cared about the community and were concerned only for themselves. Each was doing his own thing, to the ruin of Israel. The social responsibility of the old individualist was almost zero, so that he could build an industrial empire on the flayed bodies of the workers. The sense of community of today's therapeutic man is secondary to his fascination with his own needs. Responsibility to a society is a lost cause if a man spends his psychic energy trying to find and express himself.

The final reality of any society is a demand that goes beyond doing one's own thing. A community assumes that a man is not a law unto himself, an entity unrelated to others. If a man chooses to belong to a group, he loses some of his independence, and since he cannot really exist unto himself, he cannot finally understand himself without the demands of a community. John Donne wrote that every man is "a piece of the continent, a part of the main."

The philosophers have some fancy phrases for the problem of the community and the individual. For example, they speak of "internal relations" and "external relations." Internal relations are those in which the various parts of a system cannot exist without each other. A finger cut off from a hand is no longer a finger. It becomes a piece of dead flesh and decays. External relations are those in which the parts can exist apart from each other. A camshaft and a piston can be removed from an automobile engine and still remain a camshaft and a piston. Others can be installed and the engine still function. The modern assembly line functions on the principle of external relations.

Sometimes a person feels externally related to a group and at other times internally related. If one tends to move in and out of relationships with no sense of loss, the relationships are probably basically external. The IBM card is an example of the force external relationships can have. When a person finds a mistake on his computerized bill, he may eventually get quite frustrated trying to settle the matter by communicating with a machine which is capable only of external relationships. He will feel much better if he can finally get through to a supervisor who understands the problem. He will feel that at least he is moving into something of a relationship.

Traditional American individualism, be it that of the nineteenth-century entrepreneur or the contemporary swinger, is a social philosophy built upon the shaky foundation of external relationship. The tug-of-war between external and internal relations is always going on within modern life. The conflict over the liberalization of divorce laws is really a conflict about the nature of marriage. Those opposing this liberalization hold to a view of internal relations in marriage; its advocates think of marriage in terms of external relations.

In a time of great mobility people more and more tend to favor external relations, as a means of protecting themselves from the ravages of broken relationships. With each move friendships are severed, and often the pain is too great to bear repeatedly. The result is a withdrawal from internal relations in favor of the less demanding and less painful external relations. It goes without saying that people who are afraid of close relationships prefer external relations. Conversely, some people who have been so emotionally starved by a diet of external relations that they crave intimacy try to make all relationships internal. They tell their innermost secrets to a service station attendant and reveal their heartaches to any indifferent ear.

Part of the pathos of modern America is that the

more industrialized and technological it becomes, the more power the society possesses and the more impersonal it becomes. Concurrently, the better educated people become, the more they become aware of their uniqueness and troubled by their loss of individuality. A country just emerging into modern society can turn out cars that all look alike and no one cares too much because everyone is grateful for the cars. But once the society develops, people become less enchanted with look-alike locomotion.

As the tension between the impersonal force of society and the awareness of personal uniqueness grows, people also become more afraid of personal relationships as their mobility increases. The result is a lashing out for fulfillment and authenticity which for the most part refuses to come to terms with the central issue. The old-time entrepreneur was externally and impersonally related because he was of the opinion that he was conquering the world. The modern swinger doing her thing is not conquering but clutching. She is trying to wring out a little self from an impersonal society.

The current fascination with sex is a pathetic attempt to find instant intimacy in a society where people are mostly objects in a mechanistic system. When people speak about the need for community, they are bearing not very mute witness to the fact that most people today are lonely, because they are externally related. Sex can give the illusion of relationship, but the reality often is that both male and female are nothing but objects.

No man can be an island entire of himself. If one tries, then one must live a lie, and the corrosion of living a lie makes one all the more imperiled. The essential problem facing a modern man is to develop the ability to remain a person in an impersonal society — an impersonal society that is gaining power as its tools and techniques become more effective. The only way a person can have this ability is to develop himself in the context of a community, because there is no way he can make it on his own. That path is not only ineffective, it is also destructive. The swinger doing her own thing really doesn't become more of a person but an easy victim of an overwhelming impersonal power. The labor union movement arose when it dawned on the workers that they could not bargain independently with the managers. Their strength rested in a community. The alcoholic cannot contend with his problem by himself. It is simply too big for him. He must have the support of a community like Alcoholics Anonymous.

The debonaire disciple lives within a convivial company, a community of faith. His awareness of the gracious presence of God in his life comes through his fellow believers. One of the cardinal doctrines of the Reformation was the priesthood of all believers. The function of a priest is mediating the presence of God, and within the church each member mediates the presence of God to the other members. The experience of God's presence comes through experience with others. Human beings do not have some spiritual sixth sense. They have the five senses, and therefore God uses the five senses. When God chose to reveal himself to man, he did it within the limits of man's flesh. He became a man. If man were able to transcend his fleshly limitations, the incarnation would not have been necessary.

The church as the body of Christ is the continuing presence of Christ in the flesh. This does not mean that the church has exclusive territorial rights on the kingdom of God. As a matter of fact, it does not refer to denominations and institutional churches. It means that the presence of God in Christ is mediated through a community of fellow believers. "For where two or three are gathered in my name, there am I in the midst of them" (Matt. 18:20).

This is not really such a strange notion. It is simply saying that God uses people to get his message across. His presence is known through the five senses. A man hears the word preached, he smells and tastes the wine and the bread at the Lord's Supper, he feels the press of the flesh of fellowship, he feels the water of baptism, he sees the symbols of the faith. The voices, the smells, the sounds, the feel of community are the means.

The inner change that moves a man to become a believer may take place deep within his experience. Hidden in the psychic corners of his being are the longings, questions, agonies, and joys that move a man to see himself in a new way. But if it were not for the visible symbols of communication, the change could never take place, for it is through these visible symbols that the invisible realities deep in the heart are fed with the inheritance of the faith.

The debonaire disciple is free enough from care to know that he needs others. The independent individualist is still something of a spiritual adolescent. He still thinks that he doesn't need anyone, and he can only sustain that illusion by a fabrication. Freedom for the adolescent is "getting away from it all." It is essentially a negation. But freedom only occurs when a choice is offered, and making the choice inevitably limits the independence. Freedom and independence are not synonymous. In fact, they have little in common, for freedom is the choice of relationships and responsibilities. Until a man is free of the burden of independence by the grace of God, he is never free enough to know that he needs others.

Oddly enough one of the groups in American life which holds most fiercely to the illusion of individualism is the medical profession. Understandably enough its members resist any bureaucratic or governmental influence in their practice of medicine. In order to maintain their integrity and protect their incomes, they resort to independence, forgetting that for the most part their education was the gift of either a taxpayer or an endowment, and that they practice in hospitals supported largely by others, and that they in fact belong to one of the most heavily supported professions in American life.

The medical profession is used as an illustration because its situation is so obvious, but in fact for almost everyone in modern life the situation is substantially the same. Very few pay for their education as they get it, and if they think that they do, they forget the vast support of educational institutions by taxes and private gifts. The values that guide a man's life he receives from others. The relationships that sustain and encourage him are the gift of others. For bedsteads, automobile engines, toothpaste, and many other things, external relations may make sense, but for the real business of living they are an illusion. The quickest way to get done in by the overwhelming weight of modern society is to live the lie that a man can make it by himself. The surest way to loneliness and isolation is always to do one's own thing.

The convivial company is that fellowship in which God encounters a man with his graciousness and his claim. His message and presence are personal, not impersonal, and so persons are the only vehicle available to him. The individualist collides with others throughout his life. The debonaire disciple engages others. He has the freedom from care to know that he needs others. In these terms the church is not an organization or a denomination. The structures of the church are only secondary and derivative. The heart of the church is that convivial company through which God reveals himself to men.

Since the community of faith is essential to the life of faith, the question is immediately raised about the life of the church. For some the church is a place of moral improvement. For others, it is a place where deep feelings are stimulated. And for still others, it is a place where the right ideas are taught and enforced. All of these definitions have nothing to do with the biblical faith or the tradition of the Reformation. The primitive Christian church described in Acts seems to have been distinguished by the Lord's Supper and the preaching of the word. The Reformer picked up this theme, and it has been the general definition of the church among Protestants. Some Protestants have thought that the sacraments and the preaching of the word were "means of grace" by which God came to man. However, this is really to mistake the meaning of the church. The church is a community of people where Christ is present, and he is present through other people. Preaching and the sacraments are not the means of his presence; they are the means of the celebration of his presence. They only have authenticity when in fact Jesus Christ has chosen to be there.

The life of the church, then, is at heart the celebration of God's presence in Jesus Christ, and the church exists on the promise that its Lord will be there. It cannot assure his presence, but it believes in it. In this sense it lives by faith and not by knowledge. The questions of doctrine, morals, and feelings are all subordinate to the celebration. The debonaire disciple may begin at the cross, but he finds himself in that convivial company which celebrates both the cross and the empty tomb. It is in this context that he is nourished and sustained, because it is in this context that the gracious presence of Christ is made known.